THE PRACTICE
OF
TEACHING

THE PRACTICE
OF
TEACHING

Philip W. Jackson

Teachers College, Columbia University
New York and London

Published by Teachers College Press, 1234 Amsterdam Avenue, New York, N.Y. 10027

Library of Congress Cataloging in Publication Data

Jackson, Philip W. (Philip Wesley), 1928–

    The practice of teaching.

    Bibliography: p.
    Includes index.
    1. Teaching. 2. Teaching—Case studies. I. Title.
LB1025.2.J3 1986   371.1′02   86-1911

ISBN 0-8077-2811-X (cloth)

ISBN 0-8077-2810-1 (paperback)

Manufactured in the United States of America

91 90 89 88 87   2 3 4 5 6

To Rose Babboni, Cora Stevens, Edith Siddons, Theresa Henzi, Nellie Campbell, Ester Bovard, Harold Wilson, Helen Walker, Arthur Jersild, Irving Lorge, and Millie Almy—teachers all, remembered with gratitude and affection.

*In the opinion of fools it is a humble task,
but in fact it is the noblest of occupations.*

—Erasmus

CONTENTS

ACKNOWLEDGMENTS

The initial version of all but the final chapter of this book was made possible by a grant from the Spencer Foundation. I am especially indebted to H. Thomas James, former President of that Foundation, for his patience and understanding. He not only allowed me much more time to complete the manuscript than had been planned at the start, but also permitted me to deviate so far from my original proposal that the final product barely resembles what I initially set out to do. Would that the heads of all funding agencies were as tolerant and sagacious!

Drafts of most of the chapters were read and criticized by Marie Schilling and Michael Smith. While benefiting immensely from their perceptive comments, I accept full responsibility for whatever weaknesses and imperfections remain in the manuscript.

Earlier versions of Chapters 2 and 5 were delivered as lectures, the former at an annual meeting of the John Dewey Society, the latter as an R.W.B. Jackson Memorial Lecture at the Ontario Institute for the Study of Education. I am grateful to both organizations for the opportunity to present those materials before public audiences. An earlier version of Chapter 6 was presented as my vice-presidential address to Division B of the American Educational Research Association at the annual meeting in Chicago in 1985.

Finally, I wish to thank Martha Harris and Yvette Courtade for putting finishing touches on the manuscript as they supervised its transition from floppy disk to typescript. Their high standards resulted in their catching many small errors that I had overlooked. The finished product is noticeably better than it would have been without their effort.

INTRODUCTION

The six chapters of this book were written as separate essays over a period of several years and in a somewhat different order than the one presented here. Thus they do not cohere as might the stages of an argument, nor does their story unfold as smoothly as a narrative whose parts follow an established chronology. Instead, they are like solitary wanderings across a broad field of discourse, six lines of travel whose paths often cross and even parallel each other for considerable distances before once again parting and going their separate ways.

Yet, as a collection, the chapters are unified nevertheless, beyond the obvious fact that all deal with some aspect of teaching. For one thing, they share a common spirit. They all treat teaching respectfully, which is to say they treat it as being important, as an activity to be taken seriously, not only by its practitioners but by the world at large. This does not mean that the stance throughout is uncritical of all that teachers say and do, but such criticism as does occur is aimed chiefly at those who erroneously belittle teachers and teaching, whether knowingly or out of ignorance.

Something else that binds the chapters together, though not too far removed from the attitude of respectfulness just mentioned, is the conviction that teaching is more complicated than most people think, including—strange to say—many teachers. Why so large a number of people should have such a view of teaching is the central question addressed in Chapter 1; the answer given is that an overly simplified conception of what teachers must know about their craft rests on a few key assumptions whose validity is quite untrustworthy. Similar questions having to do with the deceiving simplicity of teaching recur throughout the book.

In Chapter 2 they take the form of examining what William James thought about teachers and teaching and then asking how he might have come to such a view. In the case of James the situation is made more interesting by the discovery that he was not entirely forthright in letting his true opinions about teachers be known to the audiences he addressed, a precaution taken for a very good reason, it turns out.

Also, his own technique as a lecturer reveals James to have known more about teaching than he professed.

Chapter 3 addresses some of the uncertainties teachers face, which also turn out to be greater than is generally understood. Techniques for putting those uncertainties to rest, such as asking questions in class or giving tests at the end of a course, are examined with an eye to asking not only how well they serve to resolve uncertainty but also what other consequences they might have that would discourage teachers from using them. The goal of that examination is not to advise teachers on what they should do with respect to classroom questioning and the giving of tests. Rather, it is to understand why so many teachers do not employ such practices as often as they might otherwise; this apparent oversight causes them to be thought of as irresponsible or irrational (or both) by today's advocates of "educational accountability," and other forms of practice designed to ensure the objectivity of what are commonly referred to as the "outcomes" of education.

Chapter 4 treats the complexity of teaching in a different light entirely. It does so by asking whether teaching can ever be defined once and for all. Can we, in other words, ever be entirely sure whether or not a person is teaching by comparing what he or she is doing against some standard definition of what teaching entails? Anticipating the fuller argument contained in that chapter, I acknowledge here that my answer to both questions is no; but such a brief response does not begin to do justice to the complexity of the subject, nor does it contain the slightest hint of how much fun the process of speculating about such matters can sometimes be, a discovery I once made on my own.

The central questions of Chapter 5 have to do with the idea of progress as it relates to teaching. They ask whether teaching has improved over the years and, if so, whether we might expect it to continue to do so. These too turn out to be more complex questions than many people think they are. They are made so in part by the usual difficulty of trying to establish criteria of progress and by the equally difficult, if not impossible, task of projecting past and present trends into some unknown future.

But the task is made even more complex by the presence within the teaching profession of two competing traditions, each of which seeks to preserve its own definition of what teaching is all about and where it should be headed. Those two traditions, referred to in Chapter 5 as the "conservative" and "liberal" outlooks, are so thoroughly entwined throughout the history of teaching, as they are

throughout the history of human affairs in general, that it is prac-
tically impossible to trace the twists and turns of each. In fact, even
the task of naming them is difficult, for each tradition is so multi-
faceted that it answers to several names, none of which proves
adequate to the whole.

Because it comes last, Chapter 6 confronts head-on this ultimate
source of the complexity of teaching—its apparent duality. It does so
by seeking to describe in greater detail than in Chapter 5 the two
dominant outlooks on educational thought and practice. Then it proceeds to explore the relationship between them. Once again, the goal
is not to prescribe to teachers and others how they ought to think and
act, so much as it is to outline the apparent alternatives and then to
ask whether and where a choice between them needs to be made.

Finally, whom is this book for? It is written for everyone who
cares about teaching, which I would like to believe includes us all. But
I hope its principal audience will be made up of practicing teachers—
inside and outside of schools, colleges, and universities—plus their
colleagues-to-be, those who aspire to join that noble occupation,
either today or in years to come.

1 ON KNOWING HOW TO TEACH

WHAT MUST TEACHERS KNOW ABOUT TEACHING? What knowledge is essential to their work? Is there a lot to learn or just a little? Is it easy or difficult? How is such knowledge generated and confirmed? Indeed, dare we even call it knowledge in the strict sense of the term? Is not much of what guides the actions of teachers nothing more than opinion, not to say out-and-out guesswork? But even if that were so, what of the remainder? If *any* of what teachers claim to know about teaching qualifies as knowledge (and who dares deny that some does?), what can be said of its adequacy? How complete is it? Does much remain to be discovered or do the best of today's teachers already know most of what there is to learn? And whether the bulk of it is fully known or yet to be discovered, what, if anything, must be added to such knowledge to ready the teacher for his or her work? In other words, is there more to teaching than the skilled application of something called know-how? If so, what might that be?

This spate of questions, to which others of a similar nature could easily be added, has to do with the form and content of what shall be referred to here as the epistemic demands of teaching. The qualifying adjective, *epistemic*, is intended to set apart one set of occupational demands—those having to do with the knowledge teachers must have—from others that alternatively might command the attention of someone seeking to understand the task of teaching in its totality. (Other extractions would include the emotional toll the job is known to take under certain circumstances, its drain on the physical energy of practitioners, the expectations that teachers be the embodiment of society's ideals, and so forth.) More specifically, the questions raised at the start of this chapter refer to the epistemic demands of teaching *as a method*, a way of doing things, rather than to an additional set of demands, also epistemic in kind, that arise from the teacher's need to master the material being taught. The two kinds of knowledge—of methods and of instructional content—are related, of course, as common sense suggests they would be, but they are by no means synonymous, as soon will become clear.

1

Questions having to do with methodological know-how, as opposed to knowledge of subject matter, may not always be uppermost in the minds of teachers as they go about their work, but they are seldom overlooked entirely. More than that, every teacher must surely have answered, at least partially and provisionally, the most pivotal of those questions: what do teachers need to know in order to teach? This has to be true, for without having done so they would be stalled in their tracks at the start and the activity called teaching could not even get underway.

Thus we may safely assume that all teachers have *some* idea of what teaching entails in the way of method, together with *some* notion of where that knowledge comes from. On this score, however, teachers are by no means alone. Indeed, if all that were needed to credit a person with having given thought to the epistemic demands of teaching were simply his having turned such matters over in his mind now and again, nearly everybody would be so credited. Considering the part teaching plays in our lives, we can quickly see why.

In America today, as is abundantly evident, nearly everyone goes to school from age five or so onward. From the very first day of that experience our store of knowledge about teachers and their work begins to build. By the time our schooling is complete, the tally of our face-to-face encounters with teachers runs into the thousands. That extended acquaintance, whose product makes up something that might be called "school sense," leaves many people believing that they too, though not teachers themselves ("mind you," they might add), have a pretty good idea of what the job entails in the way of knowledge and skill. They may even go so far as to claim that they could teach quite well themselves, if they but tried.

Moreover, although formal schooling is obviously the chief source of such notions, it is by no means the only one. Teaching, as we all discover while still very young, is not confined to schools. We encounter it in all kinds of settings—at home, on the street, in churches and synagogues, in doctors' offices, and on the playground, to name but a few. As a consequence, our cumulative knowledge of what it takes to be a teacher is derived from many different kinds of experiences with teachers of many different sorts.

Each of these contacts with a teacher in action provides us with a glimpse, albeit one-sided, into what teaching is all about. For most people in today's world, that glimpse, repeated again and again for years on end, is sufficient to engender and sustain strong and enduring beliefs about teachers and their work.

However, despite the ubiquity of teaching as an activity, there is no uniformity of opinion about it. Thus, though almost everyone might think he or she has the answer to most of the questions raised at the start of this chapter, it would be quite wide of the mark to say that everyone agrees on what those answers should be. On the contrary, when it comes to teaching and what it entails, disagreement, rather than agreement, turns out to be rife.

In response to our opening questions, some people contend there is a lot to know about teaching; others say, very little. Some argue that whatever there is to know is easily learned, others say the task is very difficult. Teaching can be learned only on the job, according to some people; there is much to be learned beforehand, according to others. And so it goes. Sharp differences of opinion crop up almost invariably wherever teaching is discussed, from the family dinner-table to the public forum.

We find, furthermore, that the disputants in such matters do not always line up neatly with teachers on one side and nonteachers on the other, though a split along those lines is by no means unknown. Teachers, it turns out, often disagree among themselves about teaching and what its demands are in the way of knowledge, fully as much as do people who have never taught. Indeed, some of the sharpest disagreements of all, judging from the source and volume of today's complaints about our public schools and how they are run, appear to separate teachers working at one level of schooling— colleges and universities—from those working at another— elementary and secondary schools. Why this should be so, why there should be such divergent views of what teachers need to know, and why teachers should disagree among themselves about such matters are questions whose answers require a tracing of the boundary between common sense and specialized knowledge.

I.

Among the first things to note is how many kinds of teachers there are. Leaving aside the large number of nonprofessional teachers (most parents, for example), we are still left with an impressive variety of types, the major ones well-known.

To start, we are all familiar with the practice of classifying teachers according to the level of schooling at which they work. Preschool, elementary, high school, and college teachers (the last-named being called professors by many) comprise the most widely used categories of all. We are also used to hearing teachers referred to by the subjects they teach. Teachers of voice, physics, home economics, Latin, physical education, and countless other subjects are familiar enough to most of us. A complete list of such descriptive titles would contain almost as many entries as there are divisions within the domain of human knowledge.

Then there are many people, both within and outside the categories that have been named, who do not always call themselves teachers but who are so all the same. These include tutors, masters, coaches, trainers, counselors, lecturers, public speakers, professional consultants, and discussion leaders. A special subgroup is comprised of priests, preachers, and rabbis in their instructional roles, not to mention gurus and sundry other holy men. Also to be included are alpine guides, animal trainers, tour directors, certain TV performers, and recreational advisers at seaside resorts.

The duties of many of these people go far beyond teaching, true enough, but their work remains pedagogical in character all the same. So the variety of people properly called teachers, *professional* teachers to be more precise, is very great indeed. Examples range from TV's Julia Child to the professor of neurosurgery at the nearby medical school, from the lady who teaches flower arranging at the local "Y" on Saturday afternoons to the Visiting Fellow in the Department of Paleontology at Harvard. This being so, we may reasonably suspect that the divergent opinions about the epistemic demands of teaching may be related to the variety found within the occupation itself. There are so many different kinds of teachers and so many different teaching situations that uniformity in this regard is hardly to be expected. Even if we remove from consideration some of the exotic examples that have been named, we still might expect considerable variation in what teachers of quite different subjects working in very different settings will need to know about teaching.

With such differences in mind, let us now ask: can anything be said about the epistemic demands of teaching based solely on what we know to be true about how people become various kinds of teachers in our society today and how they have done so in the past? Common knowledge about such matters provides us with two interrelated observations, each bearing directly on the set of questions with which we began.

The first is that formal instruction in pedagogy *per se* is largely, but not exclusively, confined to persons training to become either elementary or secondary school teachers. Not only is this true today, but it has been so for some time, perhaps for as long as there has been such instruction.

Students preparing to teach at the college level and beyond

seldom enroll in education courses of any sort along the way. Nor are most of them given instruction within the confines of their own academic departments on how to teach the subject matter in which they are specializing. The same is true for many, if not most, teachers who work in settings other than schools. They too are unlikely to have studied teaching methods in any formal way.

Julia Child, for example, has probably never taken a course on how to give cooking lessons, much less one on teaching in general. Nor is she at all unusual in this regard. She is just like the neurosurgeon at the medical school, who in all probability has never formally studied the pedagogy of his or her craft either. The same is probably true of the lady who teaches flower arranging at the local "Y" and the Visiting Fellow in the Department of Paleontology at Harvard. None of them is likely to have studied teaching in an organized and deliberate way.

What this absence of formal study means insofar as the epistemic demands of teaching are concerned we have yet to explore, but it obviously means something. In trying to understand its significance, we must not overlook the fact that college and university teachers on the whole enjoy a higher status in the eyes of the public at large (and in the eyes of educators as well, we might add) than do teachers who work at lower levels of schooling. This difference is also reflected in the respective salaries of the two groups.

The second observation about how teachers typically are trained, or not trained, in their craft calls attention to the fact that even for elementary and secondary teachers formal training in pedagogy is a relatively new requirement. Until quite recently—within the last hundred years or so—there were very few teacher training institutions as we know them today. Even books on pedagogy were not all that numerous. In generations past people undertook to become teachers of the young solely on the strength of what they themselves had learned in school, often before completing the equivalent of today's twelfth grade, and without benefit of anything approaching the kind of training for the task undertaken in a modern teachers' college or even the kind provided in many of today's liberal arts colleges.

This situation resembles what has taken place in many other occupations and professions. All kinds of crafts and professional skills now taught in schools of one sort or another were once learned on the job, either independently, through a process of trial and error, or dependently, through some system of apprenticeship. Many are still learned that way.

For school teaching, however, as for law, medicine, and most other professions and semiprofessions, the norm has now become a training course in a college or university, typically requiring several years to complete. However, in the case of teaching, unlike most other professions, the old pattern still prevails here and there. In our independent schools in particular—both parochial and secular—one can still find a sizable number of elementary and secondary teachers who have had no official course work in education. Such "untrained" teachers, if they may be so called, are fewer in number nowadays than they once were, true enough, though there are some signs that their number may increase if the teacher shortages anticipated within the next few years actually materialize. Be that as it may, that they exist at all poses a continuing challenge to all mandates governing what courses public school teachers must take in order to be certified. Moreover, another note about status must be interjected here as well, for the truth is that many of the schools continuing to hire teachers without formal training in pedagogy are considered to be among the very best in the country.

Thus all claims about what teachers need to know in order to do their work are confronted at the start with a double paradox. They first must take into account the somewhat puzzling fact that the most prestigious class of teachers in our society—those working in colleges and universities—devote less time to the formal study of teaching than do their less respected colleagues who work in elementary and secondary schools. Indeed, those who might be considered the "stars" of the teaching profession, the world's most distinguished lecturers and professors from Socrates forward, have rarely studied the process of teaching at all in any formal sense.

After coming to grips with that set of circumstances, those who argue on behalf of requiring teachers to take some education courses before they begin to teach must also confront the additional fact that even at lower levels of schooling some elementary and secondary teachers—often in the best of schools at that—seem to get along quite well without any formal training at all. Moreover, history reveals that all teachers were similarly "handicapped" in the not-too-distant past; yet they too seemed to manage somehow. What do we make of this? How are such facts to be interpreted?

From the standpoint of teacher education in general, the harshest interpretation of the facts cited is that they add up to a sweeping indictment of the entire enterprise. "How can such programs be worth much," the interpreter of those facts well might ask, "when it is precisely the teachers who work in some of our very best schools and who teach the most advanced and complicated subjects in our colleges and universities who seem to get along quite well without them? If, of all teachers, these in particular—the cream of the crop, one might say—can do without formal courses on how to teach this or that, why can't the rest of them? The only impediments seem to be certification and other legalistic requirements, most of which look suspiciously like forms of job protection for the crowd in power."

This line of criticism is fairly common within the academic community at large and has been for some time. In the next chapter we will see it at work near the turn of the century in the correspondence and writings of no less illustrious an academician than Harvard's own William James. For the time being, however, it will suffice to say just a word about the scope of the criticism.

Though the primary target of our hypothetical critic's charges is obviously that much maligned category of practitioners known variously as "teacher educators" or "teachers of teachers" (the latter ascription often delivered with mocking intent), the impact of the criticism is by no means restricted to them alone. Though not its primary target, elementary and secondary teachers are tarred by the same brush. They are so by virtue of being associated with an educational enterprise of dubious worth.

This is the harshest reading of the reality of countless untrained teachers working in colleges and universities and in many good private schools throughout the land; it is undeniably incomplete, as so brief a sketch must be. Yet even in its brevity it should suffice as a recognizable depiction of the way some people actually think. How many no one knows, but probably quite a few.

As a comment upon the epistemic demands of teaching, that line of thought has several important shortcomings. The first is that it addresses those demands indirectly at best. From the observation that many teachers seem to get along quite well without formal training, the conclusion is drawn that all or most other teachers might do so as well. But the fact that some teachers can go without formal training says nothing about what teachers in general need to know. It certainly does not prove that there is little to learn about how to teach. All it asserts directly is that apparently not everyone needs to take courses on the subject of teaching (and perhaps read books about it) in order to perform reasonably well in the classroom. Which teachers can safely go without such training and which others cannot is a question the facts themselves do not address. Also they leave the door wide open to the possibility of learning through direct experience, informal interchange with teaching colleagues, and so forth. Of course, the people making use of such facts usually are doing so to denigrate the notion of teachers' needing to know much of anything beyond the actual subject matter they teach. Consequently, the facts are intended to *insinuate* that there really *is* little to learn about teaching. Like all insinuations, however, they stop short of saying what those who employ them want others to conclude. Thus, as an argument against there being a lot to learn about teaching, observations about the number and quality of untrained teachers leave a lot to be desired.

The second shortcoming of such observations is that they ignore the phenomenon of *unsuccessful* teaching and why it happens. The question here is, if learning how to teach is really as simple as the evidence seems to imply, why do people fail at it? There are many ways of answering that question without introducing epistemic notions—for example, it may be that unsuccessful teachers suffer from some kind of emotional deficit—but until the phenomenon is addressed head-on and the epistemic alternative discarded, there remains the strong possibility, vexing to those who think there is little to learn about teaching, that many such teachers are best explained as simply lacking in know-how.

These and other weaknesses aside, we still must deal with the facts on which the criticism rests. To avoid interpreting them in a way that is highly critical of teacher education programs and, indirectly, of the teachers who pass through them, we must seek other interpretations. A favorite interpretation among those teacher educators who bother to address the question makes use of the idea that there are compensatory qualities of one sort or another enabling teachers with little training, or even none at all, to make up for their deficiency.

John Dewey, for one, favored this view. He acknowledged that there are some teachers who, as he put it, "violate every law known to and laid down by pedagogical science."[1] What makes such teachers effective? They are so, explained Dewey, because "[t]hey are themselves so full of the science of inquiry, so sensitive to every sign of its presence and absence, that no matter what they do, nor how they do it, they succeed in awakening and inspiring like alert and intense mental activity in those with whom they come in contact."[2]

Thus, Dewey posited a superabundant "spirit of inquiry" that was capable of making up for a lack of pedagogical knowledge. Others, using the same underlying logic, have nominated qualities

---

[1] Reginald D. Archambault, *John Dewey on Education* (New York: Random House, 1964), 330.
[2] *Ibid.*

like enthusiasm and empathy to play an equivalent role in their explanatory theories.[3] What this line of reasoning reduces to is the contention that there are, in a word, "born" teachers, whose abilities are such that they either instinctively behave correctly when placed in a teaching situation or, as Dewey puts it, behave in such a way as to compensate for whatever else they might be doing that could be judged wrong. These naturally endowed teachers, we are asked to believe, are the ones who get by and even excel without formal training.

The chief difficulty with all such *post hoc* theories lies in their circularity. We begin with the observation that some teachers seem to be doing quite well without training, and we proceed to explain that "anomaly" by ascribing to such persons some special powers or gifts. How do we know they are so endowed? Because we observe them doing well despite a lack of training. We can avoid this logical deficiency if we are sufficiently careful, but to do so requires an independent test of the explanatory hypothesis, a move seldom made by those who, like Dewey, put their views forward not as hypothesis but as established fact.

Another difficulty with these compensatory theories is that they usually are designed to deal with special cases, whereas the phenomenon of teachers without formal training, at least in colleges and universities, is the rule rather than the exception. Unless we are prepared to entertain the possibility that *all* such teachers, or nearly so, are blessed with one or more of those special talents believed to overcome a lack of training, theories of the kind suggested will not cover sufficient ground to do the job required.

The most serious difficulty of all, however, is that all such theories beg the question: Are there truly, as Dewey claimed, "laws known to and laid down by pedagogical science"? If so, what might they be? Indeed, is there any such thing as a "pedagogical science"? Dewey must have believed there was, or he would not have used the term as he did. But was he correct? We certainly don't find the expression in wide use today. Why not? The most sensible explanation I can think of is that the term is pretentious when used to describe what we today can say with confidence about how to teach. But if a pedagogical science has not yet been achieved, is it still reasonable to hope that one day it will be?

---

[3]See, for example, Barak Rosenshine, "Objectively measured behavioral predictors of effectiveness in explaining," in Ian Westbury and Arno Bellak (eds.), *Research into Classroom Processes* (New York: Teachers College Press, 1971), pp. 51-98.

Such questions begin to sound suspiciously like those with which we began, and so they are. They return us to the central task of establishing what teachers need to know and where they get their knowledge. We must now do so, however, in the light of the observations that have been made about untrained teachers, without jumping to either of the conclusions proffered so far—the one being that there really is no such thing as pedagogical knowledge (or something close to that), and the other that such knowledge, lawful in structure and scientific in character, not only exists but demands mastery by all would-be teachers, save perhaps a small number who are specially gifted.

II.

Let's begin afresh by granting one of the underlying assumptions of many people who belittle the importance of pedagogical training: that the knowledge teaching calls for draws heavily on common sense. Let's agree that it does. That may seem like too great a concession to make to the foes of the entire concept of pedagogical knowledge, but we quickly see it is not when we consider that the same could be said of most other human activities as well. Indeed, when we stop to think of it, we quickly realize that common sense, roughly defined as knowledge picked up in the course of living, is crucial to the performance of everything we do.

Not only does it serve as a guide to action in all our endeavors, it also provides, through the medium of language, the concepts and categories that make reality intelligible. It gives meaning to experience. It speaks authoritatively in both descriptive and prescriptive terms, telling us not only what *is* but also what *ought to be* with respect to all manner of things and situations.[4] Given its vital role in human affairs in general, we should hardly be surprised to find common sense crucial for teaching as well.

What does common sense say to teachers? What does it tell them to do? First of all, it obviously says a lot that has little or nothing to do with teaching *per se*. It provides the teacher with the meaning of all common objects, like chairs, tables, walls, doors, cats, dogs, and so forth. The voice of common sense also tells them things like, "Bundle

---

[4]For a provocative discussion of the complexity of common sense, see Clifford Geertz, "Common sense as a cultural system," *The Antioch Review* 33, number 1 (Spring 1975): 5-26.

up when it's cold," "Come in out of the rain," "Put your left shoe on your left foot," "Don't touch hot stoves," and so many other commands that any attempt to list them would be folly.

This kind of rudimentary knowledge and elementary advice about how to behave probably does not contribute directly to a teacher's effectiveness in most teaching situations, but we can easily imagine how its absence could be a real handicap, great enough to interfere with teaching itself. Because such an unfortunate event rarely happens we may quickly pass over the portion of common sense that forms the bedrock of human understanding but does not, of itself, bear directly on the teacher's task. We are still left with plenty to think about, however, for common sense contains a lot more than information about everyday objects and injunctions about how to behave in ordinary situations.

Much that it provides bears upon the professional activities of teachers in no uncertain terms. It tells teachers things like, "That's what a person looks like who wants to say something," "There's a look of surprise," "That's an expression of disbelief," "There's a nod of understanding," and so forth. It further tells teachers, along with the rest of us, to speak in a clear voice, to write legibly, to listen when others are speaking, to ask questions when puzzled, to smile when pleased, to frown when displeased, and much, much more about how to "read" the behavioral cues of others and how to respond to them in a manner that is at once understandable and socially acceptable.

Common sense also speaks in sterner tones from time to time. As the voice of conscience, it tells teachers to keep their promises to students; to be considerate of those who are having difficulty with the material being taught; to express thankfulness for cooperativeness and other expressions of goodwill; to be truthful; to persist in the face of adversity; to avoid behaving in a way that might corrupt the morals of youth; and, again, much, much more about how to govern one's actions, not simply in the interest of communicating with others and being understood by them, but also as a way of contributing to loftier goals like justice, harmony, and humaneness.

Having gone only this far in explicating what common sense might be thought to include and how its various components might contribute to a teacher's performance, we are prepared to draw two conclusions. The first is that common sense, as here defined, is absolutely essential to the teacher's work and is so in a nontrivial way. Any lingering doubt about that proposition present at the start should by now be gone. The actions of teachers, like those of everyone else, are constantly responsive to that vast and largely unarticulated network of shared understanding that comprises much of what people mean when they talk of common sense. The dictates of that invisible web of cultural constraints and sanctions are what make social exchange, and thereby teaching itself, possible. Within classrooms, as within the world at large, the strictures of common sense are seldom violated without cost.

But it should also be clear from the examples given thus far that, costly or not, the dictates of common sense are not always obeyed. This is the second conclusion pressing for recognition. Most of us know to bundle up when cold, to ask questions when puzzled, to persist in the face of adversity, and to do most of the other things that common sense tells us. The truth is, however, that we do not consistently act on that knowledge.

Why not? For a variety of reasons. Sometimes we are forcibly prevented from doing so. Sometimes we just plain forget. Sometimes we willfully and even perversely disregard what common sense tells us to do.

When the latter happens we often wind up having to preface our explanation of what happened by saying something like, "I knew better than to do that, but . . . ." Thus, even though its role in teaching may be large, the mere possession of common sense is not sufficient to assure that teachers everywhere and always will behave commonsensically.

There is an additional point that must be inserted here. It is that common sense, when it speaks imperatively, is not always of one voice. It tells us to be prudent and cautious, but it also advises us to strike while the iron is hot. It tells us to ge gentle in our dealings with the young, but it also warns us not to spare the rod, for fear of spoiling the child.

This contradictory nature of common sense means that the simple formula of listening to its dictates and doing what they say will clearly not do. What teachers (and everyone else as well) often need is some way of deciding *which* voice of common sense to heed.

Can common sense itself deliver us from such dilemmas? It's hard to see how it can. What seems to be needed in all such situations is something more on the order of "good" sense, as opposed to "common" sense, though it is not at all clear what the former concept entails and how it differs from the latter. What this means for teaching is quite straightforward. It puts to rest, once and for all, the simple-minded insistence that teachers need only pay attention to common sense in order to do a good job.

To continue our exploration of how common sense contributes to teaching or, as seems now the better way of putting it, how it could *potentially* do so, we need to restate an observation made at the start: that nearly everyone, which logically includes nearly every teacher, has as part of his or her store of experience an acquaintance with teachers and teaching stretching back to the beginning of his or her days in school. Whether that experience is properly viewed as being a part of common sense is hard to say, for as we have already seen, what the term covers is by no means clear. The case on its behalf, however, seems strong enough to me.

The near universality of the experience of going to school would seem to put our memories of school life in the same class of mental "stuff" as that containing most of what goes by the name of common sense. But even if that should turn out to be an unacceptable argument, it is perfectly clear that the knowledge culled from prior experience in school is there as a potential resource to be drawn upon by all who face the demands of teaching.

What does that knowledge provide the would-be teacher? It provides him or her with some notion, vague though it may be, of how to do many of the things teachers do—how to use blackboards, assign homework, correct papers, construct tests, conduct exams, give grades, lead discussions, deliver lectures, monitor seatwork, pass out materials, and more. It provides information about how teachers deal with recurrent crisis situations, such as those created by unruly students or by students who persistently give wrong answers to the teachers' questions. It provides memorable instances of what happens when teachers seek to wield their authority and are challenged in doing so. In short, it provides a set of norms for the would-be teacher, a veritable scrapbook of memories about how teachers in the past have acted and, therefore, how one might oneself act in a similar situation.

At this point, advocates of today's teacher training programs, and perhaps all fair-minded critics of those programs, might well object that many of our most enduring memories of our schooldays are based on experiences with "old-fashioned" teachers or teachers of poor quality and are therefore not fit to be used as guides by anyone teaching today. They doubtless have a point. But two observations must be made in response.

The first is that a poor or old-fashioned guide is still a guide, like it or not. The primary question being addressed here is not: Where might untrained teachers turn for the *best* advice on how to teach? Rather, it is: Where might they turn for any advice at all? Professional educators may complain to their hearts' content about the quality of the average teacher, past or present; but there can be no doubt that everyone who undertakes to teach anything comes equipped, for better or for worse, with a built-in encyclopedia of pedagogical information contributed by teachers he or she has known in the past. Whether that encyclopedia should be consulted or ignored is a question totally distinct from the sheer fact of its existence.

The second, and more important, observation is that in all likelihood much of what the experts would consider to be poor teaching, and therefore not to be tapped from the storehouse of memory, we recognize as such without the aid of expert opinion. Most people do not remember simply that teacher X did this and teacher Y that. They also recall liking teacher X and disliking teacher Y. They remember that X made the subject interesting and Y made it dull, X was fair and Y unfair, and so on. The practical conclusions drawn from such memories may not be as refined and sophisticated as those offered by today's experts in pedagogy, but they are clearly far from worthless, all the same.

In addition to being exposed to both good and poor teaching, or at least to some better or worse than some other, most of us probably have also been exposed to more than one form or style of both kinds. Restricting ourselves to memories of what we took to be good (judgments with which even the experts would probably agree), we recall some teachers as superb lecturers, others as excellent discussion leaders, and still others as being at their very best in one-on-one tutorial sessions. Some teachers impressed us with their wit, others with their honesty, still others with their erudition. Some of our favorites were firm, others relaxed and informal. In sum, the memories of each of us doubtless attest to the fact that good teaching is not one way of acting, but many ways.

The point just made is similar to the one already put forward about the contradictory nature of common sense. It says that even if we could count on everyone possessing a mental scrapbook full of faded memories of teachers past, we could not assume that such memories simply lie in waiting, ready to be used whenever we need them. How they are drawn upon and put into practice is a question much like that of deciding how to extract "good" sense from "common" sense.

Summarizing what has been said so far about the contribution of past experience in school to pedagogical know-how, we would begin by pointing out that to teach as one remembers having been taught is an option open to everyone. Teachers who lack formal training, such as those working in colleges and universities, may have no other option to consider. Even those who have been systematically introduced to other possibilities may still prefer the way they remember having been taught themselves. Nonetheless, whether they use it or not, the way of teaching prescribed by their "school" sense (the latter a sub-division of "common" sense) remains a resource to be drawn upon by all teachers, trained and untrained alike.

Thus it turns out that common sense alone, broadened to include the outcome of having witnessed many teachers in action from childhood onward, equips our would-be teacher with a lot of what he or she needs to know in order to do what the job demands. Indeed, if anything, it tells the teacher *more* than he or she needs to know about certain aspects of the work, in that the teacher is confronted with not one but two or more commonsensical ways of behaving. Given this abundance of advice issuing from common sense alone, we might well ask whether anything else at all is needed when it comes to what teachers must know. Why, in short, look elsewhere?

As a prelude to addressing that question, two reminders are in order. We first must recall that our concern throughout this chapter is with the *epistemic* demands of teaching, leaving aside, at least for the time being, all other attributes, psychological and otherwise, that teaching might call for. This means that even if we were to discover that all of teaching calls for little more than the application of common sense we would still not be allowed to conclude that everyone who possesses common sense is capable of being a teacher. That conclusion would be questionable for the simple reason that it overlooks the possibility of there being other qualities that teachers must possess, beyond knowledge *per se*, if they are to do their job well.

We must also recall that an additional epistemic demand of teaching, beyond the purely pedagogical, was acknowledged at the start. This was the teacher's need to have mastered the material to be taught, a demand said to be related to his or her knowledge of how to teach that material, but not identical with it. Now it is time to examine that relationship somewhat more carefully. The central question is whether the knowledge of any teachable subject or skill, from astrophysics to basket weaving, entails a certain amount of pedagogical knowledge as well. In other words, if a person knows something, does he or she automatically know how to teach it?

A partially affirmative answer to that question has already been given for knowledge that is itself a product of actual teaching, which doubtless covers a sizable amount of what most people know. A person who has been taught anything, we have just finished noting, has presumably witnessed the teaching of that subject and thereby has some memory of the event to use as a guide in any future teaching he or she might undertake. That observation would seem to go a long way toward answering the question of where pedagogical knowledge comes from.

However, in addition to ignoring knowledge that does *not* come about through teaching—skills picked up through trial and error, for example, or the kind of worldly wisdom credited to the sheer process of living—the notion of gaining pedagogical knowledge through watching teachers in action does not really address the question being asked: Does knowledge of all kinds, regardless of how it was acquired, contain within itself directions about how it might be transmitted to someone else? Does, say, a chemist's knowledge of chemistry or a tennis star's knowledge of tennis tell her anything about how to teach what she knows to others, independent of how she herself may have come upon that knowledge?

Most people would answer yes to this question, but not with equal assuredness and not all for the same reason. Some would do so because for them school teaching is essentially a game of show and tell. In this view, to know something or to know how to do something is tantamount to knowing how to teach that something. All the knowledgeable person need do, this line of reasoning concludes, is to pass the word along, show-and-tell style.

The chemist who knows the formula for some chemical compound need only display that piece of knowledge in the presence of his or her students in order to teach it to them. (For the slow learners in the class the formula might have to be repeated a few times, granted, but the basic principle remains the same.) The tennis instructor need only grasp the racquet properly and show the position of his grip for the attentive novice to see at once how it is done. The same holds true for scores of other skills. Even without a word being spoken, many of them can be taught in a twinkling through the simple process of demonstration.

From this perspective, every kernel of knowledge and every unit of skill might be said to contain within itself a pedagogical imperative of the sort that says, "Tell me or show me to someone else if you want to pass me along." Such a conception of the teacher's task is appealingly simple; that much must be granted. Moreover, it is basically correct. Many teachers are indeed "show-ers" and "tell-ers" a good portion of the time. Some may even insist that that's all they ever are. Who is to call them wrong?

Usually, however, teaching involves much more than either

showing or telling in the narrow sense of either term, which is to say simply demonstrating a skill or reciting an assortment of facts. The process of learning calls for more than that too. Typically, students are called upon to do much more than merely parrot back what the teacher says or mindlessly mimic what he or she does.

Beyond memorization lie other forms of learning, most of which depend upon the creation of conditions of conscious consent that go by names like understanding, appreciation, comprehension, realization, and the like. To establish these conditions teachers are constantly required to give reasons, to explain, to justify, and, generally, to provide rational support for what is being taught. Thus, the trouble with the show-and-tell conception of how knowledge guides pedagogy is not so much that it is wrong as that it does not go far enough. As a perspective on the whole of the enterprise, it stops short of what we need to take into account if we are to ground our educational efforts in a modern view of knowledge and an updated conception of human mentality.

To correct these shortcomings we first need to recognize that facts seldom exist in isolation, nor do we usually present them to students in that way. They are parts of large wholes, or rather more grandly, they are elements within enveloping frameworks of epistemic significance. Physical skills too, particularly those taught in school, exhibit the same kind of relatedness. Typically, they are shown to be linked, one to the next, in some overall strategy or plan of action.

We refer to these epistemic superstructures by a variety of names, calling them things like bodies of knowledge, systems of thought, fields of study, intellectual disciplines, domains of inquiry, sciences, arts, crafts, sports, games, and so forth. Each such term refers to something holistic. It stands for a more or less distinct and distinguishable unit of human understanding. Each, therefore, refers to something that can be studied and taught in an organized way. Thus, from a pedagogical point of view, the *relational* and *contextual* aspects of facts and skills—their place within their respective frameworks—often turn out to be fully as significant as the facts and skills themselves. Indeed, it has been argued by some educators—Jerome Bruner, for one—that the lineaments of these larger structures are more important to impart to students than is the more substantive knowledge housed within.[5]

---

[5] Jerome S. Bruner, *The Process of Education* (New York: Vintage Books, 1960).

We next need to see that the organizing principles of those over-arching assemblages of knowledge—the system of categories that divides them into parts, together with the generalized understand-ings that define their limits and hold the parts together—are enor-mously varied. Different fields of knowledge, to choose one of the broadest of the more general terms, are partitioned in different ways. In some, like history, the dominant organizational scheme is chrono-logical; in others, like anthropology, geographical or biological cate-gories might have a larger ordering role. Some areas of study, such as contemporary literary criticism, might be difficult to map at all, save with idiosyncratic notions like "schools of thought" or "major fig-ures." For some domains of knowledge the crucial distinction is between concepts and facts, for others it is between theory and its application. Logic looms large as an ordering principle in some fields of study, but not in others.

And so it goes. Each discernible structure of knowledge or reper-toire of skillful performance is laid out according to a plan of some sort whose gross outline and features are generally familiar to people considered to be experts in that particular domain. However, the way such plans are drawn varies immensely from one field to the next. Let us assume that these structures and their organizing principles are of some pedagogical significance, without pausing at this point to con-sider what that significance might be; we see at once that teachers of some subjects are very likely more advantaged than others in having at their disposal, for whatever pedagogical purpose it might serve, a firm and well-defined conception of how their domain of expertise is organized.

We must also note that in many fields of knowledge there is no single, universally agreed upon "structure" at all. Instead, there are alternative ways, some hotly contested, of bringing order to what is known. The competition among such organizational schemes is clear-ly evident in school and college textbooks in many subjects.

What this means pedagogically is that teachers are often faced with a choice of frameworks within which to couch their efforts. (This point is very much like the one made earlier about the plethora of advice issuing from common sense.) Thus the simple dictum: "Teach what you know" is made complicated by the fact that what one knows usually can be presented to students in a variety of different ways.

A recognition of this condition would seem to move us very close to a type of know-how that is both central to the teacher's work and unequivocally pedagogical in nature: *the knowledge of how to organize knowledge for teaching purposes.* If that organization is in any way different from the way knowledge is organized for *other* purposes—that is, for handy reference by people who are already experts on the subject or skill in question—it would seem like a piece of pedagogical know-how teachers could not do without.

The proposition that knowledge need be specifically arranged for teaching purposes seems sufficiently incontrovertible to be considered a truism. But the truth of that proposition does not succeed in moving us into a new domain of epistemic demands facing teachers. For when we begin to think of the principles that might guide a teacher in readying knowledge for delivery to students, we find ourselves returning to the arena of common sense. In other words, at least many of the principles we encounter are sufficiently a part of almost everyone's way of looking at things to make them as commonsensical as they are pedagogical.

One such principle, for example, would be to proceed from the easy to the difficult. Another, related to the first but not precisely the same, would be to move from the simple to the complex. A third, useful when narrating events that can be arranged chronologically, would be to start at the beginning and continue on to the end. A fourth would be to move deductively, from the logically prior to the subsequent. And so forth.

The listing of such pedagogical rules of thumb appears to return us to our earlier observation that common sense contains most of what people need to know when called upon to teach something to someone. If following such rules is all there is to it, it begins to look as though the critic's view was right after all. Even when we move from common sense in general to pedagogical principles in particular, teaching continues to look as easy as rolling off a log.

Or does it? Are the easy and the difficult readily distinguishable throughout the universe of teachable knowledge? In some fields, like mathematics and certain of the sciences, they certainly seem to be, but even there—as in the question of which is more difficult, algebra or geometry?—we are often not sure. And what about the simple and the complex? There we find the same thing: the two are not always readily distinguishable. Consider, further, all the decisions that narration calls for. It's one thing to know that beginnings always come before endings, but knowing that tells us nothing about how much detail to include or how to build dramatic tension or any of the other things a good narrator needs to know. Even the sanctions of logic do not provide infallible guides. The prior comes before the subsequent when proceeding deductively, true enough, but is deduction superior to induction when presenting material to be learned? Again the answer seems to be: sometimes, but not always. So, though common sense may point the way, even when it comes to something as pedagogical as how to arrange material for presentation to students, we once again must note that it cannot be relied upon to function automatically, nor is the advice it gives always the best available.[6]

By this time it will have occurred to some readers that nothing has been said to this point about one very important element in all teaching situations, namely, the person or persons being taught. Here surely is a source of information for making pedagogical decisions that must be fully as important as the material being taught. Teachers need to know a lot about the students they teach in order to teach them properly. What could be more obvious?

Though that conclusion *sounds* sensible enough, it turns out to be false. The truth is that many teachers seem to get along quite well without knowing much at all (in the extreme case, nothing!) about the students they teach. Who those teachers might be and how they might get along quite well without such knowledge are questions whose answers move us closer to understanding why some kinds of teaching might make epistemic demands that others do not. They also serve to introduce some thoughts about pedagogical mishaps of one kind or another.

One group of teachers who characteristically get along with very little information about the students they teach are those who do their teaching via television or radio. They do so, it seems, by substituting three key assumptions for what other teachers and common sense itself might deem it essential to know. When these assumptions are valid, as they often are, teaching proceeds quite smoothly, although the teacher does not know anything at all for certain about his or her students. When, on the contrary, those assumptions are *in*valid, as they sometimes turn out to be, teaching either falters as an enterprise or comes to naught.

The first of these assumptions, rarely necessary in most teaching situations, is that there actually are students witnessing the teacher's actions or at least listening to his words. This assumption, which is

---

[6]Many teachers never trouble themselves at all with decisions about how the material they are teaching should be presented to their students. Instead, they rely upon commercially prepared instructional materials such as textbooks to make those decisions for them. Even so, they are often faced with the task of choosing from among the many materials available, as has already been said, and the criteria for making *that* choice almost inevitably include some that would be considered pedagogical in nature.

absolutely crucial for all radio and television teachers who are not working with a live audience, we will call *the presumption of a public*. For teachers who meet their students face-to-face, as most do, such a presumption is hardly called for. There the students sit in plain view of the teacher and of anyone else who might come upon the scene. There is of course the possibility that the students who are present are not actually attending to what is being said and done by the teacher. That condition, as we know, is not exactly unknown. But commonly it affects only a portion of the teacher's audience, so that in almost all face-to-face teaching situations the assurance of a public, even if a small one, is present at the start and need not be presumed.

The crucial point is that without an audience of some sort, either visibly present or presumed to be out there somewhere, the activity of teaching would lose its meaning. A person going through the motions of teaching in an empty classroom with no TV cameras or microphones around is not actually teaching at all. What we want to describe such a person as doing—rehearsing for teaching, perhaps, or trying imaginatively to recreate a teaching episode that had taken place in the past—will depend on the circumstances; it certainly will not be called teaching as understood either historically or contemporarily.

The second assumption that teachers of invisible audiences have to make in order to give sense to what they are doing is that some if not all of their students are in need, in purely epistemic terms, of whatever it is that is being taught. For short, let's call this the *presumption of ignorance*. Considered by itself, the presumption of ignorance does not necessarily entail the belief that is often associated with it: that the missing knowledge is essential to the definition of a well-educated person or a competent worker (or whatever) and, therefore, must be supplied. In other words, there need be no corollary assumption that the missing knowledge is essential, even though that assumption is often tacitly asserted as well. For the presumption of ignorance to work all that need be assumed is a gap of understanding or skill, capable of being filled at least in part by what the teacher does or directs his or her students to do. Without either assuming or knowing that the students in question are in need of instruction, teaching would be a redundant undertaking and therefore a waste of time.

The third assumption is more difficult to describe than the first two. It has to do with the similarity between the teacher and his or her students. For this reason I call it *the presumption of shared identity*, though what is meant by that phrase is not immediately apparent and the phrase itself may be a trifle misleading. One aspect of what is shared with students, or is assumed to be by most teachers, is summed up by the expression: "our common cultural heritage." What that heritage contains is rather difficult to say with precision, but certain of its contents are clear enough. It includes a common language and a large part of the kind of commonsense knowledge about which much has already been said. It includes a knowledge of cultural heroes, popular tastes, and everyday customs and conventions, all of which enable people to feel at home and to behave understandably within a specific cultural context.

Another aspect of the presumption of shared identity has to do with psychological functioning. Acting on this presumption, teachers take for granted that their students are like themselves in the way their minds work, in the way they think and feel, in what makes them laugh and cry, and so forth. This includes an assumed similarity in physiological terms as well, in such things as the factors that create fatigue, how much stress can be tolerated, the conditions that bring on excitement or boredom, and so forth. In short, the presumption of shared identity implies the existence of a match between teachers and students along several dimensions at once: cultural, psychological, and physiological.

Such an assumption effectively frees the teacher of the need to inquire into the nature of his or her students as a guide to making pedagogical moves. It enable him or her to teach, almost literally, with eyes closed. Should a question arise, for example, about whether students might find a particular piece of instructional sequence interesting or boring, the teacher need search no further than the boundaries of his or her own consciousness for an answer. Does he find the material interesting? Then, on the presumption of shared identity, he may rest assured that his students will do the same. To the extent that the presumption is justified, he need have no further worries on that score.

There is one more requirement for the teacher who lacks direct knowledge of his or her students, either by choice or because it is unattainable. Beyond having to presume that there really are students out there to be taught (essentially, only for those teachers who literally cannot see their students), that they are ignorant in ways that might be rectified by teaching, and that they are more or less like the teacher in many fundamental ways, the teacher must also have some indication of how long instruction should continue in both the short-term and the long-term sense. What he or she needs, in other words, are ways of knowing when to terminate instruction, without relying on information from students to make that decision. The requirement, in short, is for an *a priori* set of exit rules.

In many teaching situations this is quite possible to do without establishing such rules in advance. Instead, the teacher may rely upon more naturally occurring signs that it is time to stop work. For example, the teacher might keep an eye out for signs of fatigue among her students. Alternatively, she might monitor her own feelings of stress and strain for signs of when to call it quits for the day. Instead of deciding in advance how many teaching sessions to have, she might choose to continue teaching until her own knowledge runs out, until she can truthfully face her students and say, "Now I have taught you all I know," or something to that effect.

In reality, of course, teachers seldom go that far. Nor do they wait until fatigue shows among their students to terminate individual lessons. Instead, whether forced to do so or not, they commonly settle upon a more or less standard and somewhat arbitrary unit of time as the length of a single teaching session or "lesson," and they space such units with considerable precision and regularity within large blocks of time. The result is the familiar: "Typing I will be taught on Tuesdays and Thursdays from 4:30 to 6:00 PM in Room 109." They also commonly establish in advance (or have it established for them) the overall duration of instruction, either tying it to a particular date—for example, "classes will end on June 12"—or limiting it to a specific number of sessions, as in "ten easy lessons."

As these examples make clear, establishing exit rules—usually quite arbitrary ones—is not a procedure limited to teachers who know very little about their students. On the contrary, teachers of all kinds rely on rules of this sort, even those who give private instruction and thereby come to know each of their students very well indeed. The chief reason for introducing the idea of exit rules within the present context was to round out the total set of conditions enabling some teachers to make do with very little in the way of direct knowledge of their students (in the extreme case, none at all) yet at the same time manage (if all else is in their favor) to do a good job of teaching.

Having completed that "rounding out," at least in a preliminary way, we are now in a position to look back on what has been said so far about the sources of pedagogical knowledge. The main points that have been made return us to the barrage of questions introduced at the start.

III.

We began by acknowledging that a sizable portion of what teachers need to know is available to them in that vast storehouse of knowledge known as common sense. We next noted that common sense for most people includes the cumulative residue of a long acquaintance with teachers and teaching, begun at the start of formal schooling, if not before then. To that was added the observation that knowledge itself contains pedagogical imperatives of one sort or another, having to do with both the content and the structure of what is being taught. Finally, we saw how, under certain circumstances, teachers might make do with very little direct information about the students they are teaching, relying instead on three key assumptions, plus a set of more or less arbitrary conventions for bringing instruction to an end.

The three assumptions were (1) *the presumption of a public*, (2) *the presumption of ignorance*, and (3) *the presumption of shared identity*. The conventions for terminating instruction were said to be covered by *a set of exit rules*.

Now it is time to ask what all this says about what teachers need to know in order to teach. Initially, we must admit that much of what has been said appears to buttress the argument of those who belittle the notion that there is much to learn about teaching. Common sense, which includes knowledge of how schools work and of what teachers do, does provide the teacher with much of what he or she needs to know much of the time, which is precisely what a lot of the critics of teacher education have been claiming all along. Add to that a thorough knowledge of the material to be taught and we seem to have gone a long way toward answering the spate of questions with which we began.

But this is by no means the whole story, as we have also seen. As soon as we begin to spell out what common sense entails and start to acknowledge the multiplicity of forms that knowledge can take, the superficiality of the claim that teaching is nothing but applied common sense becomes readily apparent, as does the equally simplistic notion that it entails nothing more than displaying one's knowledge in the presence of students.

When we see how teachers might be guided by common sense, we can also see how they might be boxed in and frustrated by conflicting advice from that quarter. The pedagogical imperatives embedded in knowledge seldom turn out to be as straightforward as the show-and-tell conception of teaching would have us believe. Instead, we find teachers continually being called upon to tailor what they know to fit the needs, interests, and abilities of the students with whom they work, a task that calls upon considerations above and beyond those derived from the materials being taught.

Some teachers, we acknowledged, seem to get along quite well without knowing much of anything about their students as individuals—Julia Child of television fame, as a prime example—but we also saw that the success of those who do so would seem to depend on the validity of a few critical assumptions, any one of which, if invalid, could either derail all instructional efforts entirely or render them meaningless.

Moreover, a close examination of each of these assumptions reveals that we can never be absolutely certain of their appropriateness, chiefly because we can never know for certain what's going on in the minds of anyone save ourselves. (Efforts to discover what students *really* think about something or what they may be said to know about this or that present a set of unique problems for teachers, as will become clear in Chapter 3.) So, though it might be reasonable and even necessary for teachers to assume quite a bit about what their students know or do not know in order to get on with the business of instruction, the possibility of error in making such assumptions is widely acknowledged, as are its consequences. Teachers who *think* their students are with them when they are not, who assume ignorance when there is none, who envision their students as being carbon copies of themselves, when in fact they are quite different, are obviously courting failure; the irony is that so long as they cling to their erroneous assumptions they may never find out they have failed.

At this point a few critics might insist that the discussion so far appears to wind up just about where they predicted it would from the start: a strong confirmation of the belief that teaching depends on little more than common sense plus knowledge of the material to be taught. In epistemic terms alone, this viewpoint concludes, teaching is quite easy. But that is not really the point of the discussion thus far at all, or at best it is only part of the story.

Common sense is essential for teachers (and for everyone else!), as is knowledge of the material to be taught, but the combination of the two is hardly sufficient to guide the actions of all teachers everywhere, as some of the examples I have given should suffice to make clear. Even the most commonsensical and erudite of teachers is sometimes faced with the necessity of making choices and taking actions without the help of guidelines from either domain of knowledge, the everyday or the academic. Such situations call for hard thought. The advice of colleagues may also prove helpful.

Therefore, if when he calls teaching "easy" the critic means "not requiring much thought" or "not intellectually demanding," it seems rather clear that the critic himself has not thought very much about all that teaching entails. But what about teaching as "easy" in the sense of "not much to learn in the way of pedagogical principles, facts, techniques, and so forth?" Is the critic at least correct on that score?

The answer would seem to be yes, but with one very important qualification. The principles of teaching, or the "laws of pedagogical science" as Dewey called them, do seem few in number and not all that complicated either, *provided the presumption of shared identity is validly held*. In other words, when teachers are working with students *who are very much like themselves*, there is relatively little to learn about teaching, at least insofar as technique is concerned, that is not supplied either by common sense or by knowledge of the material to be taught. But when teachers and students are *not* alike in important ways—that is, when the presumption of shared identity is *in*valid— there may be quite a lot to learn about how to proceed. The knowledge called for under those circumstances is genuinely knowledge about teaching *per se*. It is not a part of what most people would call common sense, nor is it deducible from knowledge of the material to be taught. Instead, it has to do with such things as the developmental characteristics of students and how to adapt instructional procedures in the light of those characteristics, how to handle social situations involving the potential for conflict, how to proceed in the face of disagreement over the purposes and goals of instruction, and so forth.

The enumeration of situations calling for "pedagogical" knowledge, as opposed to common sense plus what might simply be called erudition, gives rise to an important question about the presumption of shared identity. Quite simply, it is: Can such a presumption *ever* be validly held? Is it true that no two people are exactly alike? That being so, doesn't everyone who presumes a shared identity with others— teachers no less than anyone else—run the risk of being in error at least part of the time? Therefore, why presume a shared identity to start with? Why not begin with the assumption that the teacher and her students do *not* fully share the same outlook on life or the same psychological makeup or the same anything else and move forward from there?

The answer, it seems, is that some form of the presumption of shared identity must remain unquestioned, at least temporarily, for social interaction to become a possibility. That is, if I believe the objects before me do not even share my humanness, if they are mannequins, let's say, or some lower form of life, I may proceed to act upon them, moving them about, shouting commands at them, and so forth. But I do so in a manner quite unlike that of most human interactions. Consequently, the question is rarely whether the presumption of shared identity is valid or invalid. Rather it is: To what *extent* is it valid? What are its limits?

What this turns out to mean is simply that some teachers are more like their students than are others. The question is: Which are which?

Leaving aside the exotic category of teachers who work exclusively with animals rather than humans (dog trainers, horse handlers, circus performers, and so forth), surely the greatest difference separating teachers and students is that of age. Most teachers are adults; most students, children. It follows, therefore, that some knowledge of what children are like, what things appeal to them, what the limits of their understanding might be, and so forth comprises the major epistemic ingredients of what teachers of the young must know.

Where does such knowledge come from? How is it acquired? The answers to those questions will surely vary from teacher to teacher, but some practical experience and formal training—the former including directed observations and practice teaching, the latter including courses in child development—doubtless are the norm for most teachers who have gone through a standard teacher training program in this country within the past few decades.

But what about the untrained elementary and secondary teachers mentioned at the start of this chapter? How do they manage without this essential component of pedagogical knowledge? Or do they?

The answer seems to be that some people gain an understanding of children in the course of living that others never do. Jobs as baby-sitters and camp counselors must certainly play a role for some. So too must experience with younger brothers and sisters. But however it comes about, it turns out that some adults are more comfortable in the presence of children and enjoy their company more than do others.

For such persons the usual kinds of introduction to the world of childhood provided by most teacher training programs would probably add very little to what they already know. This is not to say they have nothing to learn from developmental and cognitive psychologists like Vigotsky and Piaget. The point is simply that such knowledge is not likely to make them feel more at ease with children than they already feel.

Teachers and students differ in more than age, of course, and sometimes these other dimensions of dissimilarity turn out to be very significant as well, more so at times than age itself. Differences in social class, for instance, are widely acknowledged to be a hindrance in the communication between teachers and students. So too are differences covered by the standard variables of race, ethnicity, sex, and physical handicaps.

A teacher's failure to take such differences into account can be the source of difficulty in many a tale of pedagogical woe. But at the same time, this is not invariably true. Differences between teachers and students in any or all of the aforementioned variables are often irrelevant to what the teacher decides to do. The question of whether they are or are not relevant seems to depend chiefly on what is being taught.

What this comes to in the end is the realization that the question of what teachers need to know about their students in order to teach them properly cannot be answered for all teachers everywhere. Some need to know more than others, that much seems obvious. At the same time, a few broad generalizations do seem to be in order.

One is that teachers of adults can usually rely on the presumption of shared identity more readily than can teachers of the young. Another is that teachers who share with their students a similar social class background have a great advantage insofar as presumed identity is concerned. Thus, college and university instructors who habitually lecture to classrooms full of very able and advantaged students can usually get by with much less knowledge about those students (of both a general and specific sort) than might, say, a kindergarten teacher with his or her class.[7] Still another is that highly routinized skills can be taught much more impersonally (that is, without the teacher's being concerned with who the students are) than can skills whose efficacy depends largely upon style or manner. The same would seem to hold true about facts as opposed to interpretations.

Differences of this kind doubtless account for some of the disagreements among teachers mentioned at the start of this chapter. For example, given the differences they face as teachers, we need hardly be surprised to find some college instructors failing to grasp the epistemic demands facing a nursery school teacher with a room full of three-year-olds. The latter, in turn, can hardly be blamed for

---

[7] This is not to say that college and university teachers do not occasionally put *too much* reliance on the presumption of shared identity. Quite frankly, I suspect many of them do, which is why students complain of teachers who "talk over their heads."

wondering how college instructors can get along without a course in developmental psychology.

Is teaching easy or difficult in purely epistemic terms? Though distressingly vague, the only acceptable answer seems to be that it is easier for some kinds of teachers than for others. Beyond knowing the subject they are to teach, teachers must possess or acquire knowledge of their students. The need to acquire this knowledge seems greatest in those situations where the teacher must take into account at almost every turn the uniqueness of the students with whom he or she is working.

To take only one of the many widely discussed differences among teachers, a debate has raged within educational circles over the years as to whether teaching should be "child-centered" or "subject-centered." Advocates of the child-centered point of view argue, in essence, that teachers in elementary and secondary schools should concern themselves more with the students they are teaching and less with subject matter *per se*. Expressed as a slogan, their view is that one should teach children, not subjects. Advocates of the subject-centered point of view, who seem to be fewer in number than their opponents, argue quite the opposite. They accuse the latter of being soft and sentimental. Though they might not go as far as to boast of teaching subjects, not children, they certainly lean in that direction.[8]

Given what has been said in the closing section of this chapter, it is easy to see why teachers of the very young are more likely to be "child-centered" than "subject-centered." The latter point of view gains sympathizers as we move up the grades. However, it should also be clear at this point that the debate is focused on what is really a false issue.

First, the expression "student-centered" should replace "child-centered" so that the issue is broadened to cover all of teaching.[9] Second, the question that really needs careful examination and perhaps public discussion as well is: When is it appropriate and neces-

---

[8] For a clear and fair-minded treatment of that subject, see Harold Entwistle, *Child-centred Education* (London: Methuen, 1970).

[9] All, that is, save for a rather exotic group of teachers who work exclusively with animals. It is not entirely clear what to call animals who are being trained or taught by humans, if indeed they require any special name at all. To refer to them as "students" seems a bit odd, yet in a sense that is what they are. "Subjects," the terms scientists use to refer to animals (and often humans as well) when reporting on their experiments, sounds a bit more appropriate, even though regal in tone. Perhaps the absence of any special designation suggests there need be none.

sary for teachers to be sensitive to the students' characteristics and when not? The two extreme answers—always and never—can be eliminated at the start.

Finally, we must ask where this discussion of the epistemic demands of teaching has taken us with respect to questions having to do with the usefulness of methods courses and other practical experiences—such as classroom observations and student teaching—that comprise a large part of the curriculum of many teaching training programs. In the light of what has been said in this chapter, are such courses and training experiences largely a waste of time, as critics have sometimes charged?

There is certainly no way of answering that question without a look at each program; however, it should be clear from what has been said that many teachers might gain much from those portions of their training curriculum that help them think about how particular materials and skills might best be arranged and presented for pedagogical purposes. Critics who claim that all such knowledge is simply a matter of common sense are surely wrong. At the same time, the fact that such courses *could* be useful does not make them so. In the final analysis, teachers themselves must judge.

2 HOW TO TALK TO TEACHERS: LESSONS FROM WILLIAM JAMES

DURING THE SUMMER OF 1892 WILLIAM JAMES delivered a series of public lectures on psychology to the teachers of Cambridge, Massachusetts. He did so at the request of the Harvard Corporation. Why the request was made is a fact now shrouded in mystery, though plausible explanations are easy enough to invent. It might well have been part of a larger public relations campaign aimed at enhancing the image of Harvard as an institution devoted to the public weal. It could also have had something to do with the fact that many children of Harvard faculty members were enrolled in Cambridge schools. What better way to generate good feelings between the University and neighboring schools?

In any event, no matter why he was asked to do so, the important point is that William James did indeed accept his university's invitation to address the teachers of Cambridge. His commitment to the task was total, amply revealing that combination of erudition and literary style that had already won him an enduring place among America's men of letters by the age of fifty.

His lectures, in all, fifteen in printed form, must have been well received by the Cambridge audiences who first heard them, for word of their popularity spread rapidly. During the ensuing years James delivered the same set of lectures, with slight modifications, to several audiences throughout the land. In 1899 they were finally published, first in installments in *The Atlantic* and later in a single volume entitled: *Talks to Teachers on Psychology: And to Students on Some of Life's Ideals*. It is in this form that his lectures are still available to the modern reader.

And well might we turn to them today, despite their age. For they contain quintessential Jamesian prose—not the most profound of his writings, most would agree, but rich, all the same, in metaphor and anecdote—infused with wisdom and enlivened by good humor. Thus, strictly as a kind of William James sampler, his *Talks to Teachers* promises enjoyment anew to those readers within each succeeding generation who want a chance to savor the diction that so thrilled audiences back in the days of horsehair sofas with mahogany legs.

For professional educators, however, there is an additional reason for turning today to what James wrote some ninety years ago. We do so because the task James faced, that of talking to teachers in a manner that might prove helpful or at least interesting to them, is prototypic of the more massive undertaking that today confronts the sprawling domain of teacher education. Those of us involved in that enterprise—professors in colleges and universities, specialists in in-service training, supervisors, administrators, and, of course, teachers themselves—may be said to be embarked on a Jamesian quest. For we too, in a manner of speaking, are out to discover how to talk to or with teachers in ways that might somehow help them as they go about their work in classrooms.

By looking at how William James responded to that challenge, by pausing to reflect on his rhetoric, by pondering his choice of words, and in particular by teasing out some of the tacit attitudes and opinions that guided his pen (and perhaps misguided it as well, as we shall soon see!), we shall hope to return home with a fresh perspective on the larger enterprise in which we are collectively engaged. We turn to James, then, as an aspiring young artist might turn to a study of the Masters, seeking not so much to be told exactly what to do as to be stimulated, perhaps even inspired, to move the process along a step or two further. What we hope, in other words, is that a close look at how he set about his work will stir thoughts that will give either a new impetus or a new direction to our own efforts.

This spirit of critical inquiry dictates that we be less concerned with the academic content of James's remarks, his turn-of-the-century psychology, than with the less visible assortment of assumptions, opinions, prejudices, and other forms of thought that lie half-buried beneath that content, supporting and giving shape to the whole. If we are lucky, our probing of these underlying beliefs, this bedrock that juts up here and there like shadowed outcroppings throughout James's lectures, will do more than yield information about the man who wrote *Talks to Teachers*. It should also prompt us to dig into the substratum of our own thoughts about teachers and teaching, for we too rest our efforts on foundations that are not always exposed to the light of self-scrutiny.

A good example of what I am here calling the bedrock of James's thought surfaces in the very first paragraph of the Preface to his work. Before all else he makes mention of what he has learned as a result of delivering his talks to countless numbers of teachers. "I have found by experience," he confides to his readers, "that what my hearers seem least to relish is analytical technicality and what they most care for is concrete practical application."[1] While preparing his lectures for publication, James carefully heeded that voice of experience, doing his best to weed out the technical, leaving in as much of the practical as possible. Through this painstaking process he fashioned a version of his talks designed to have maximal appeal to teachers. In their final version the lectures, as James himself described them, "contain a minimum of what is deemed 'scientific' in psychology, and are practical and popular in the extreme."[2]

For a man of James's stature and seriousness of purpose, his giving in to popular taste was not to be taken lightly. He anticipated that such a decision would be misunderstood by many of his colleagues. He even predicted that a few of them might openly disapprove of what he was doing. "Some of my colleagues may possibly shake their heads at this," James ruefully acknowledges, "but in taking my cue from what has seemed to be the feeling of the audiences I believe that I am shaping my book so as to satisfy the more genuine public need."[3]

Though we may applaud James for his courage to act in accord with what he took to be a "genuine public need," notwithstanding the criticism that such action might occasion, we must not overlook the social and psychological distinctions embedded in his prefatory remarks. Those distinctions were present in James's thinking as he composed and delivered his lectures. They continue to be very much with us today. Whether they should be treated as valid, either then or now, is a question to which we shall return.

For the present it will suffice to note that at the very start of his book James remarks upon an important difference between the crowds of people who attended his popular series of lectures and the smaller knot of companions with whom he exchanged pleasantries, day to day, while crossing Harvard Yard. This difference, in a nutshell, is that between teachers of the young and those who teach them in turn. When it comes to intellectual matters, the former, if we are to take James's word for it, have a taste for the concrete and the practical over the analytic and the technical. The latter, we are left to assume, prefer the reverse.

If we pass too hastily over these opening remarks in the Preface

---

[1]William James, *Talks to Teachers* (New York: Henry Holt and Co., 1899,) iii.
[2]Ibid.
[3]Ibid.

to James's *Talks* we are apt to dismiss them as trivial. On the surface at least, they are nothing but a passing comment on a difference in taste between classroom teachers on the one hand, and university professors on the other; a difference to be kept in mind when writing a book for teachers, as James himself set out to do, sure enough, but nothing more important than that. Or so it first seems. It is only when we pause to consider the reaction James anticipates from his colleagues that the significance of his observation begins to dawn.

The image of James's learned colleagues shaking their heads in disapproval and clucking their tongues in disbelief on hearing of his decision to write in a popular and practical vein is a mental picture well worth preserving. As a kind of cartoon image, it expresses better than do words an attitude toward teachers and teaching that yet today is widespread in academic circles. That attitude, by implication, raises a very serious question about the possibility of meaningful dialogue, or even one-way communication, between the university-based academician, on the one hand, and the school-based practitioner, on the other. If such talk is to go on, the wagging heads of James's colleagues warn, it must be stripped to the bone of intellectual content. Such a state of affairs is doubly lamentable, their clucking tongues inform.

It is so, first of all, because it uses up the time and energy of a man of James's stature. Why would a man such as he stoop to writing such drivel? is the tacit question they ask. It is even more lamentable, their criticism implies, when we consider that one *must* write or speak that way if one wants to communicate with an audience of teachers. "Isn't it a pity that good old James, of all people, is taking on such a task?" would be the query behind the first lament. "Yes, but how sad that teachers are so dull that they must be spoken to in such a manner," would be the observation behind the second.

The fact that James delivered his lectures and went ahead to publish them, undaunted by what he took to be the wagging heads of his colleagues, leads us to conclude that he himself did not fully share either of the two sentiments here so briefly described. Yet neither was he entirely free of them.

Writing to Professor George W. Howison of Stanford University in 1897, James had this to say about teachers.

Experience has taught me that teachers have less freedom of intellect than any class of people I know. . . . .A teacher wrings his very soul out to understand you, and if he does ever understand anything you say, he lies down on it with his whole weight like a cow on a door-

step so that you can neither get out or in with him. He never forgets
it or can reconcile anything else you say with it and carries it to the
grave like a scar.[4]

It may seem a trifle unfair to reveal these thoughts that form the
underside, as it were, of James's attitudes toward teachers. Such
sentiments were obviously not written for the world to read. Better
they should remain tucked away in private correspondence than to be
dragged out in the open this way. To do so, even from as safe a
distance in time as this, may strike some readers as being a bit un-
sportsmanly, like landing a blow below the belt. Were James himself
able to speak from the grave, he most certainly would yell, "Foul!"
Yet there are good reasons for bringing such strong opinions to
light after all these years, even though James himself might have
preferred they be forgotten. They force us to think otherwise than we
might about James's public remarks. For example, in the light of
knowing how he truly felt we may well wonder whether James's low
opinion of teachers in any way influenced his overall demeanor and
style as he delivered his lectures to them. We also might wonder if
and how that opinion affected the substance of his remarks. The fact
that he accepted the assignment of speaking to them at all and then
continued to do so year after year does seem a bit strange when we
consider that, intellectually speaking, he privately thought of the
members of his audiences as being rather like cows!
How common, one wonders, are similar opinions among today's
educational advice-givers? As our modern day William Jameses talk
to teachers or write for them, do visions of indolent cattle crowd their
thoughts? The question is raised half in jest, of course, but it is worth
keeping in the back of our minds all the same. Lodged there it serves
as a reminder of a condition sometimes forgotten, which is that many
educational issues of what appear to be a purely intellectual kind are
actually enmeshed in social and psychological complexities to which
we customarily give little attention. We ignore them at our peril.
For example, when we talk about the relationship between
theory and practice in education, we often do so in a way that can
only be called "disembodied." We speak as though both theory and
practice were nothing but abstractions whose relatedness, one to the
other, was simply a matter of deductive logic. But when we look at

---

[4]Ralph Barton Perry, *The Thought and Character of William James* (Boston: Little,
Brown and Company, 1935).

what happens in the real world, we discover that theory is the central preoccupation of one set of people and practice the preoccupation of another. In other words, the two notions are "embodied," as it were, in two quite separate groups of individuals whose interrelation-ships—as James's unflattering metaphor about teachers as cows so painfully reminds us—are not always as we might like them to be. That fact in turn sets the stage for further revelations of an equally painful sort. James's ghost may not like us to linger over his long-ago thoughts about teachers, but the imagery in which those thoughts were cast is well kept in mind as we tiptoe, figuratively speaking, into the lecture hall where the first of James's talks is about to begin.

His opening lecture, entitled "Psychology and the Teaching Art," begins with warm praise for his audience. Such an opening was probably quite standard at the time, and is still in fashion today among a certain class of public speakers, yet it is a trifle unsettling all the same in the light of what we now know James's private opinion of teachers to have been. He applauds what he calls "the fermentation" that has been going on among American teachers for a dozen years or more. In James's view this fermentation has taken the form of a kind of inward reflectiveness, "a searching of the heart," as he puts it, "about the highest concerns of [the teaching] profession."[5] Teachers everywhere, he reports, seem to be earnestly "striving to enlighten and strengthen themselves."[6] If such efforts are maintained, James predicts, "in a generation or two America may well lead the educa-tion of the world."[7]

Such lofty motives presumably accounted for the huge atten-dance at James's own lectures. For of all the advice-givers to whom teachers of the day had turned in their search for enlightenment, none, it appears, were more sought after than psychologists, among whom James stood out as preeminent. This turning to psychologists was understandable, James goes on to explain, for psychology as a field of study was undergoing a "boom" at the time. Indeed, it was so popular that it had turned into something of a bandwagon atop which all kinds of people were all too eager to scramble. Chief among the scramblers, James tells his audience, were "editors of educational journals and the arrangers of conventions [who] have had to show themselves enterprising and on a level with the novelties of the day."[8]

---

[5]James, *Talks*, 3.
[6]Ibid.
[7]Ibid., 4–5.
[8]Ibid., 6.

In their eagerness to satisfy the craving of teachers for psychological knowledge, these editors and convention planners had failed to be sufficiently discriminating. As a result, much that had been written for teachers on the subject and much told to them from convention platforms was, as James put it, "more mystifying than enlightening."[9] In hot pursuit of greater intellectual clarity, the hapless consumers of what was written and spoken—the poor classroom teachers—found themselves "plunged in an atmosphere of vague talk."[10] To make matters worse, even some genuine professors, who presumably should have known better, were contributors to this vagueness.

In the midst of describing this sad state of affairs, James tosses out a couple of observations that are themselves a trifle puzzling, if not to say vague in their own right. He notes that the fog of mystery swirling around the new science of psychology as it is presented to teachers seems also to enshroud other topics that are, as he puts it, "laid upon teachers" by those purporting to give pedagogical advice. Indeed, this blanket of fog is so thick and pervasive on the educational landscape that it appears to be almost a natural feature of the place. James calls it a "fatality," as though it were a condition that somehow *had to be*.

This condition puzzles James, for he sees nothing mysterious about teaching *per se*. Indeed, the "matter" of the teaching profession, a term he uses to refer to the knowledge teachers must master about their craft, strikes him as being "compact enough in itself."[11] Yet for some strange reason this compact subject must invariably, as James put it, be "frothed up for [teachers] in journals and institutes, till its outlines often threaten to be lost in a kind of vast uncertainty."[12]

This *is* a puzzling state of affairs, we must admit, and no less puzzling today, we might add, than when James mused upon it. Why is it, indeed, that so much of the material written for teachers and so many of the things told to them, both then and now, exude this aura of mystery, this strange kind vagueness—this fog? What is there about teaching as an activity or about teachers as persons that causes this to happen?

James does not frame the question in these terms, but he does answer it, all the same. The trouble, as he sees it, is two-pronged. A finger of blame must be pointed at both the mystifiers and the mysti-

---

[9]Ibid.
[10]Ibid.
[11]Ibid.
[12]Ibid.

fied, at the former for spreading confusion and at the latter for tolerat-
ing it. Addressing the latter first, he accuses teachers of not having
been sufficiently independent and critical-minded. "And I think," he
says, "that if you teachers in the earlier grades have any defect—the
slightest touch of a defect in the world—it is that you are a mite too
docile. . . ."[13]

Just a mite too docile. Can't you almost see the twinkle in James's
eyes as he spoke those words? Picture also the audience's response—
gloved hands raised in mock surprise, handkerchiefs masking the
beginnings of smiles. Just a mite too docile! Such a gentle chide. If
one must have a defect, what better could one wish for?

Yet, if we refuse to be lulled into inattentiveness by the sweet
sound of James's criticism, we can discern in his words an echo of the
complaint more harshly expressed in his letter to Howison. "Docile"
may sound gentle enough, all right, but what animal is more docile
than—yes, you've guessed it—a huge, brown cow with droopy eyes,
lying supine on the grass? Close attention to each word of James's
reproach reveals even more. Note that he accused the teachers in his
audience not simply of being docile, but of being *too* docile. Now if we
assume he chose his words with care—a reasonable assumption, it
would seem, in the light of all the editing and polishing he presumably did before the lectures were published—his qualifier reveals a
fundamental ambivalence toward the quality he describes in teachers.
What it says is that James did not object to docility in teachers as a
general characteristic. It bothered him only when it became excessive.
The tiny word "too" tells all. In other words, cows are okay; it's just
when they squat on one's doorstep that their docility turns out to be
something of a nuisance. Even then, better them than bulls!

Here we must pause to take stock of our own unexamined assumptions and presuppositions, for it is quite possible that our prior
knowledge of James's private opinion of teachers has made us hyper-
sensitive, causing us to pounce upon a single word, reading too much
into it. Perhaps James was not saying, "I would like you teachers to
be docile, *but not too much so*," or anything like that at all. Given our
lack of knowledge about what he truly meant perhaps it is best to
abandon that line of thought for the time being and turn, instead, to
the question of what James wanted teachers of the young to be less
docile *about*.

The answer is quick in coming. We need only to examine the
quotations already cited. James wanted teachers to be less accepting

---

13Ibid., 6-7.

of the pronouncements emanating from the so-called experts in the field of education, a group he identified obliquely as "those who get a license to lay down the law to [teachers] from above," or those "more mystifying than enlightening."[14]

Remember? Who could forget? Here, surely, is the true source of the difficulty. We may chide teachers all we like about their being too uncritical in their acceptance of the advice that comes to them "from above," but such a flaw, if it is one, clearly would not matter if what came to them from on high were itself flawless. Thus, though teachers themselves may hardly be declared blameless, the true villains of the piece turn out to be those who write and speak volumes full of nonsense that pass for educational wisdom.

Who would dispute the logic of this line of reasoning? The criminal, as we know, is always more at fault than his victim, even though the latter may be admonished for not having stayed out of harm's way. That's what James was doing. He was admonishing his audience for having been victimized. The real criminals, it turns out, then as now, are the ones who do the victimizing.

So far, so good, but before we assent to the logic of the argument we would do well to ask who the criminals in this instance, or at least the suspects, might turn out to be. Were James standing before us now, at whom would his finger of blame be pointing? The answer to tht question requires no lengthy deliberation. The true target of James's criticism was that vast army of willing workers, past and present, who have shouldered the major responsibility for preparing teachers, school administrators, and other educational specialists and who seek to provide continued support to them on the job. They are the ones James describes as having a license to lay down the law to teachers from above. Today they answer to many different titles: professors of education, teacher trainers, curriculum specialists, supervisors of practice teachers, and more. But James in his day had a shorter name for them: the mystifiers, one and all!

Nowhere in his lectures does James come right out and declare that all who teach teachers are full of bunk. He was far too much the New England gentleman to say such a thing in public, even if he believed it. Nor can I find among his published correspondence any reference to the teacher training establishment as a whole. Beyond charging that many such people are mystifiers, he seems not to have captured in a memorable metaphor what he saw as their essential character, as he did with teachers. Yet there seems little doubt that he

---

[14]Ibid., 7.

held a low opinion of the group as a whole. That opinion, like the one he had of teachers, was tainted with prejudice.

Thus, recalling James's polite chide to teachers and remembering, as well, the old saying about turnabout being fair play, we are prompted to declare that if William James had any defect at all—the slightest touch of a defect in the world—it was that he was a mite too prejudiced toward teachers and those who worked with them. Come to think of it, the word *too* can go. It only confuses things. So does the word *mite* as well. He was not a *mite too* prejudiced. He was just plain prejudiced—let's face it.

To accuse anyone of being prejudiced is a touchy thing to do under any circumstances. The touchiness increases when the prejudiced person is no longer around to defend himself or to be shown the error of his ways. After all, we can do nothing to alter a dead man's mind. Why not then drop the matter entirely?

The reason is that if we are to think straight about education we must see straight as well. And seeing straight entails an unflinching look at the way things are, whether we like them or not. Thus, although we lack the option of confronting James and trying to convince him that he was wrong, we must still face the significance of his anti-educationist views, for they were not his alone, we must remember. Many other people in his day and ours have felt the same way. How shall we deal with that opinion?

We must begin, I regret to say, by accepting the likelihood that there were grounds for James's prejudice. If anyone had bothered to challenge him, he probably could have recounted specific instances in which he had heard or read material prepared for teachers that was little more than hot air. We would not be hard put to find such material today, goodness knows. Indeed, after quickly sampling a handful of today's educational journals or attending an educational convention or two, we come away wondering if James might not have been right after all.

There *is* a lot of educational nonsense written and spoken in the name of educational wisdom these days, and we who call ourselves professors of education or trainers of teachers write and speak the bulk of it. The same was probably true in James's day. Given that fact, the low opinion widely held by professors of academic subjects toward their colleagues in education may not be a prejudice after all. Perhaps it is nothing more than a clear-eyed response to the way things are.

But such gloomy thoughts do not advance our understanding of how to rid education of its charlatans, thereby removing the grounds that give rise to prejudicial thoughts. One way out of the gloom may be to depersonalize the issue for the time being, forgetting about who, or what group, should shoulder this or that amount of blame for the way things were in James's day or are with us today. Rather than focusing on either the producers of nonsense or the hapless consumers of their product, we might better turn to the subject itself, teaching, and ask what there is about it that lends itself to such obfuscation. Whence cometh the fog? That question has the added advantage of returning us to our text.

Recall what James says about teaching early in his series of lectures. He claims that its subject matter, by which he means teaching itself and not what is being taught, is, as he puts it, "compact enough in itself." From this it follows that if our talk about teaching is in any sense complex the difficulty lies not in the subject itself. Rather, it stems from our urge to sound profound when we have something less than profound to say.

Who can deny that such things happen? Must we not also acknowledge that they do so more often than we care to tell? Many writers and convention speakers in the field of education doubtless yield to the temptation to promise more than they can deliver. There is no excuse for their doing so.

But is that all there is to it? What of the claim underpinning James's charge? Is the subject matter of teaching truly "compact," as he says? What might it mean to say so? The term itself suggests something small and neatly arranged, like a compact car or a case of cosmetics. Does such a description apply to teaching? If so, how?

Interpreted as candidly as might be allowed, the description seems to imply that all there is to know about teaching can be laid out in rather simple terms. Further, it suggests that such knowledge already exists, either in the minds of today's practitioners or written down somewhere as a set of propositional "do's" and "don'ts" that almost anyone of moderate intelligence could master within a very short time.

But how do we reconcile this set of propositions with what James says to his audience in his opening remarks? If all anyone need know about teaching were truly as simple and as tidily arranged as he implies, why then does he find the teachers of his day "striving to enlighten and strengthen themselves"? Why so much "searching of the heart"? Indeed, if there were so little to learn about teaching why would so many practitioners bother to attend a series of ten or fifteen lectures by the famous William James?

No, I fear it just will not wash. A striving of the heart and a

compact subject matter are fundamentally incompatible. They con-
tradict one another. Thus, without claiming to know precisely what
James had in mind when he called the subject matter of teaching
"compact," I am led to conclude, with some temerity, that he was not
thinking very clearly at that particular moment, despite all his
erudition and native intelligence. Moreover, I further suspect that
James himself, upon reflection, would concur with that assessment.
He was too intelligent and too honest to have refused to acknowledge
his own mistakes.

He was not *completely* wrong, as he himself might have insisted.
There *is* a lot about teaching that is straightforward and uncom-
plicated, much of it so obvious that it hardly bears attention. We have
already explored the chief dimensions of that aspect of teaching in
Chapter 1. No one needs to be told, for example, that teachers should
strive to be fair in their dealings with pupils, that they should be
well-grounded in their subject matter, that they should balance
criticism with praise, that they should be willing to admit to their own
mistakes, that they should return graded papers as soon as possible,
and so on. Such pedagogical truths, and more which could easily be
adduced, come close to being self-evident.

If such were all there was to know about teaching, we can easily
see why someone like James might describe the whole business as
"compact enough in itself." Teaching, in this view, really does look
quite simple. Almost any fool could do it.

Yet, as anyone who has taught can readily attest, there is more to
it than that. It is easy to say, for example, "Be fair with your
students." But what does fairness mean within the context of a
classroom? Does it mean treating all students alike? Clearly not.
Spending an equal amount of time on each? No. Is it fair to praise
some students and not others? Quite possibly. What about grouping
students on the basis of ability—is that fair? Well, now, . . . the
questions multiply, the light diminishes, the fog thickens.

An equally opaque cloud of uncertainty hangs over many other
pedagogical truths that, at first glance, look to be mere truisms.
Almost any one of them, if examined carefully, leads to questions
whose answers are far from obvious. The same applies, of course, to
pedagogical advice that looks rather less than obvious at the start.
The only difference is that in the case of the former the encircling
swirl of confusion is upon us all the sooner.

To choose a kind of middling pedagogical truth as a case in point,
consider the suggestion that all teachers be required to study psychology. What good, we might ask, will it do them? Let us now see

how William James himself answered that question. As we do, we must stay alert for the first layers of haze that soon will build to the foggy condition he complains of when speaking of those who hand down advice to teachers "from above." Attend carefully as the crepuscular curliques of mystification slowly rise, entwine the branches of his thoughts, and finally engulf them completely.

He is disarmingly modest at the start. He begins by declaring that all the talk of a "new" psychology for teachers to master is really nothing but hokum. "There is nothing," he asserts,

> but the old psychology, which began in Locke's day, plus a little physiology of the brain and senses and theory of evolution, and a few refinements of introspective detail, for the most part without adaptation to the teacher's use.[15]

These "pluses" are of relatively little pedagogical value, as James sees it, for, in his view, "[i]t is only the fundamental conceptions of psychology which are of real value to the teacher; and they . . . are very far from being new."[16] So much, then, for the claim of modernity that might have attracted some teachers to this field of study.

He next moves to dispel even further any unrealistic expectations that may linger in the minds of his listeners. He does so by offering a warning that has since become one of the most widely quoted admonitions in the field of teacher education. It goes as follows:

> I say moreover that you make a great, a very great mistake, if you think that psychology, being the science of the mind's laws, is something from which you can deduce definite programmes and schemes and methods of instruction for immediate schoolroom use. Psychology is a science and teaching is an art; and sciences never generate arts directly out of themselves. An intermediary inventive mind must make the application, by using its originality.[17]

To emphasize this point, James remarks on the extreme case of Johann Friedrich Herbart, who was a psychologist and who also did much to advance the art of teaching. Herbart's pedagogics and his psychology may have run side by side, James acknowledges, but, he asserts, "the former was not derived in any sense from the latter."[18]

15Ibid.
16Ibid.
17Ibid., 7-8.
18Ibid., 8.

This observation prompts James to restate in no uncertain terms the warning he has already given:

> To know psychology, therefore, is absolutely no guarantee that we should be good teachers. To advance to that result, we must have an additional endowment altogether, a happy tact and ingenuity to tell us what definite things to say and do when the pupil is before us. That ingenuity in meeting and pursuing the pupil, that tact for the concrete situation, though they are the alpha and omega of the teacher's art, are things to which psychology cannot help us in the least.[19]

So far, so good. No danger now that a teacher listening to James or reading his book would cling to the mistaken notion that the study of psychology will yield a precise set of pedagogical "do's" and "don'ts" to be put to work in the classroom. On that point he or she has been amply forewarned.

Yet, despite these cautions, James obviously believes that the study of psychology would be beneficial to teachers, even though it might not guarantee their success. In fact, he goes so far as to say that "psychology ought certainly to give the teacher *radical* help."[20] But if teachers cannot deduce definite programs and schemes and methods of instruction from the subject matter of psychology, how may it still be of radical help to them? The answer to that question is crucial not only for the defense of psychology as part of the curriculum of teacher training, but also for the defense of almost any other portion of that curriculum that does not promise a direct payoff in the development of specific teaching skills and practices. Why, in short, study *any* subject whose practical worth is not immediately obvious? The relevance of this more general question is not confined to teacher training. It may be raised with respect to any facet of education that does not have an obviously utilitarian outcome. All the more reason, therefore, to listen carefully as James frames his answer.

As it turns out, he does not give *an* answer to the question of why teachers should study psychology. He gives several. Indeed, he hurls them out in such rapid-fire order that he can only be said to pepper his audience with answers.

He first suggests that a teacher's knowledge of psychological principles may make a negative, rather than a positive, contribution

---

[19]Ibid., 9.
[20]Ibid., 5.

to his classroom performance. It does this by helping him decide what *not* to do. "We know in advance, if we are psychologists," James asserts, "that certain methods would be wrong, so our psychology saves us from mistakes."[21]

Now this *is* a bit puzzling, you must agree, for we have already heard James tell us that we cannot, from the study of psychology, deduce definite programs and methods for immediate classroom use. But if psychology cannot tell the teacher precisely *what* to do, how can it tell him with any greater precision what *not* to do? That question requires some thought. Unfortunately, James does not aid us by providing concrete examples or by elaborating on his assertion in other ways. Instead, he simply drops the matter and turns to his next point, almost as though he did not want his audience to ponder too deeply what he had just said.

His second claim for the benefits to be derived from psychological study is fully as puzzling as the first. Paradoxically, this claim has to do with clarity. Adjusting his cravat, we might imagine, and gazing with confidence on the sea of expectant faces, James bluntly declares, "It [the study of psychology] makes us, moreover, more clear as to what we are about."[22] Period. No hint is given of how this clarity is to be achieved. Nor are we ever told what the object of clarification might be. "What we are about" could refer to educational goals and purposes, but it could also refer to practices and procedures. Which of these James intends, if either, is left to our imagination. Is it not odd that a statement about clarity should be so obscure?

As with his first claim for what the study of psychology might do for teachers, the second one James mentions also begs for elaboration. But as before, he gives his audience little time for reflection before pushing on to yet a third justification. This one, in fact, is not a single reason but a trio of them, all having to do with the personal benefits to be derived from the teacher's psychological studies.

The first of these is a growth in confidence. "We gain confidence in respect to any method which we are using," James argues, "as soon as we believe that it has theory as well as practice at its back."[23] In other words, we might expect a teacher's sense of self-assurance to be bolstered by discovering that the teachings of psychology are in accord with the classroom practices *in which he or she already engages.*

---

[21]Ibid., 11.
[22]Ibid.
[23]Ibid.

This sounds sensible enough. We can easily imagine such a teacher saying something like,

> I now have two reason for behaving as I do in the classroom. I do so because I have found these methods to work, but also, I am pleased to discover, because they are in agreement with what is known about how the human mind operates.

It would be nice to have a few examples of this bolstering effect, but even without them we are not left quite as uneasy as we were when James talked about how psychology helped the teacher decide what *not* to do and how it contributed to his clarity of thought. If, indeed, the findings of psychology could be shown to be in harmony with good pedagogical practice, that news should be passed along quickly to all practitioners, especially to those who might feel the slightest bit insecure.

But this growth in confidence is not all that psychology promises to give to those who study its teachings. Nor is it, according to James, the most important of its gifts. "Most of all," he tells his audience, "it fructifies our independence and it reanimates our interests. . . ."[24]

Presumably, the independence to which James is referring here has to do with making up one's own mind about pedagogical matters, rather than relying on the opinion of others. Again, it is not entirely clear how the study of psychology will "fructify" this happy state of affairs, but no one, certainly, could wish it would not.

Finally, there is the promise of reanimation, of waking up the teacher's interests. This welcome awakening derives from a growing capacity to look at children from what James calls "two different angles" and by so doing

> to get a stereoscopic view, so to speak, of the youthful organism . . . and, while handling him with all our concrete tact and divination, to be able at the same time, to represent to ourselves the curious inner elements of his mental machine. Such a complete knowledge as this of the pupil, at once intuitive and analytic, is surely the knowledge at which every teacher ought to aim.[25]

On this confident note James brings to a close his argument on behalf of psychology as an appropriate subject for teachers to study.

24Ibid.
25Ibid.

Now what are we to make of this mishmash of warnings, claims, and promises? It brings to my mind one of those advertisements for patent medicine that cluttered the popular journals and newspapers of James's day. Picture the copy for such an ad. *Study Psychology and Have Your Mind Awakened!* it would shout. Beneath that heading would appear:

Grow in Confidence and Independence! Avoid Pedagogical Error! See the Inner Workings of Your Pupils' Mental Machines! Be the First Teacher on Your Block to Achieve Stereoscopic Vision!

Surely we must dismiss all this as pure hokum and, if we are charitable, forgive poor old James for having fallen victim to the very disease he diagnosed with such accuracy in others—systematic mystification, the common cold among our pedagogical ills.

And yet something stays us from quickly dismissing James's claims for the study of psychology. What is it that gives us pause? Is it simply the Victorian quaintness of James's appeal, the nostalgia for a day when the world was innocent enough to be taken in by such malarky? I think not. For me it has something to do with that image of an advertisement for a patent medicine.

When I think back upon those old ads I realize that the pills and ointments they sought to sell probably had little medicinal value. Most of the so-called elixirs were likely to be nothing more than treacle laced with alcohol. Yet the ailments they were advertised to cure were genuine enough, no doubt about that, hence the attraction of such come-ons to the countless readers who rushed out to buy the miracle cure or who dutifully mailed the amount requested, in the very next post.

Thus, recalling those advertisements today we may be excused at chuckling over how gullible people were in our grandparents' day. But at the same time, if we pause to think about it, we come to realize that the ads contained much that was true about the aches and pains, the worries and insecurities, that beset the readers too whom they were addressed.

Viewing James's claims for psychology in this light, we are led to ask whether they tell us anything about the teachers in James's audience or about teachers today. I think they do. An explanation of why I think so will lead us back to the broader topic with which we began: how to talk to teachers in a manner that might be helpful to them.

Think again of the promises James held out to his audience. What was the study of psychology to do for teachers? It was to help them avoid errors, to aid them in being clearer about "what they were about," to bolster their confidence, to increase their sense of independence, and to reanimate their interests. What, then, are the ailments for which these promises are remedies?

The answer is fairly obvious. By simply transforming positive terms into negative ones we emerge with a composite picture of a teacher who is guilty of having made errors in the past and who fears making them again in the future; who is fuzzy and unclear when it comes to saying what he is doing and why; who lacks sufficient confidence in his own judgment, even when he sees that what he does "works"; who leans more heavily than he would like on the words of experts and complies too readily to the wishes of his superiors. Finally, he is a teacher who is no longer interested in his work, at least not as he once was. The fires of intellectual passion and curiosity that once burned high within him are now but dull coals whose glow has all but gone.

The picture is rather grim, to say the least, and, we would hope, farfetched as well. Surely there must be few teachers, either in James's day or in our own, who suffer all those complaints at once. Many would be found to suffer none at all, we pray. The composite image is simply too ghastly to be true. It's like those horribly exaggerated sketches of sufferers that routinely appeared in the advertisements for patent medicines which I have already mentioned.

And yet, we would do well not to dismiss such a portrait too quickly, no matter how outrageously overdrawn it may seem to us. For if we but smudge the sharp outline of our profiled teacher, making it softer and hence more lifelike, the features that emerge are not so grotesque, nor so uncommon, after all. What was initially a caricature becomes recognizably real. The face that emerges through the softened outline is none other than our own.

What teacher who has ever lived has not made errors? Who does not expect to make more? Who among us is perfectly clear when it comes to knowing what he is about? Whose confidence doesn't waver from time to time? Who hasn't caught himself secretly yearning for an expert or a boss to tell him exactly what to do, to lighten the burden of decision-making and responsibility? Who, finally, has never felt the dull ache of boredom at the thought of returning to the same classroom day after day and year after year? Not I, for one, and, I suspect, not most of us.

But the fact that these complaints are so ordinary leads us to ask whether they are unique to teaching. Might they not be simply human? In one sense the answer has to be yes. For who could possibly claim that teachers have a corner on the capacity to commit errors or to be troubled by self-doubt or any of the rest of it? And yet I wonder whether there may not be something special to teaching, something making teachers of all kinds more vulnerable than usual to recurring bouts of the "heebie-jeebies," or whatever one wishes to call the total collection of discomforts under discussion. I suspect there is. This is not to declare teachers worse off in this respect than members of all other occupations. But it is at least to raise the suspicion that they may be worse off than *many* others.

Consider, as a start, the amount of uncertainty teachers face as they go about the daily business of deciding exactly what to do each step of the way in the classroom. It is all well and good to believe, as James seems to have done, that they are guided in this process by some happy combination of tact and ingenuity telling them exactly what to say and do when the pupil is before them. Certainly that must be true in large measure or they would never make it through the day. But coasting along on tact and ingenuity is like skating on thin ice. So long as you keep moving, things are fine. It's only later, when you look back on what you have done from the safety of shore or when you contemplate doing it again, that the hazards of the enterprise begin to dawn. That's when the jitters set in.

Nor is the problem of deciding exactly what to do each step of the way the only source of uneasiness for teachers. In fact, it is but the tip of the iceberg.

Instinct and common sense may be all one needs when deciding whether to call on Bill or Sam, or how to answer Linda's request for help, or when to shift the topic of the discussion. But what about those larger questions that nag at the back of a teacher's mind? Is this material really getting across to students? Is it worth spending this much time on it? Are better materials available than those I am using? How in the world can I reach those students who seem disinterested? What in heaven's name *should* a fourth grader know?

On and on they go, seemingly without end. Perplexities of this kind trouble teachers everywhere. Back in 1892 they doubtless prompted a whole auditorium full of teachers to forego whatever else they might have done in order to attend a series of lectures by the famous William James.

As we have already seen, James himself was no slouch when it came to responding with tact and ingenuity to the pupils who were before him. He sensed what was in the hearts and minds of his audience and he responded as they expected him to do. His words were far from saccharine, as we have already seen. They even took on a scolding tone, now and again. But for all that, he was doubtless forgiven. His occasional frowns, more mock than real, were clearly intended to titilate, rather than offend.

Given what was revealed at the start about James's private opinion of teachers, these comments about his style may sound as though I am accusing him of being little more than a snake-oil salesman, a hawker of patent medicine who played on the hopes and fears of teachers while secretly laughing up his sleeve at them. Though I believe there *is* an element of truth in such an accusation, I find it far too harsh a charge to level at that great man. Moreover, the thought of James as a huckster (like most public speakers) prompts us to turn too quickly from what he says and his way of saying it without extracting from his lectures the most important lesson they contain.

Back near the start, when discussing the furtive thoughts that might have been lurking in the back of James's mind as he talked to teachers, I mentioned the largely disembodied and depersonalized character of our discussion of the relationship between theory and practice in education. We seem to forget, I said, that most of what we call "theory" is produced by one set of people who pass it along to another set. We overlook the fact that the psychological relationship between the two groups helps to set the tone of the transaction. James's claims about the benefits of studying psychology prompt us to think about yet another aspect of that complex interchange.

Within educational circles it is common to speak as though the chief, and perhaps the sole, function of theory is to guide practice. James's claims for psychology remind us that this is not so. They call attention to the fact that our customary way of talking about the relationship between theory and practice is actually quite misleading.

We speak of putting theory *into practice*. But that is not what we do at all. We put theory, or whatever you want to call the ideas we transmit, *into practitioners*, where it may serve a wide variety of functions, only one of which is to guide their actions, step-by-step. In his vague talk about how psychology might help teachers, James unwittingly prompts us to think about what a few of those additional functions might be.

We talk to teachers about psychology, he reminds us, *not* to tell them what to do, as some might believe. Indeed, he rejects that goal out of hand. (His disclaimer has to be taken with a grain of salt, for despite what he says, his lectures actually do contain many helpful hints and practical suggestions.) But his warning about not being of immediate help probably did not discourage many members of his audience, for the bulk of them were not there to be told what to do in their classrooms. They came with deeper and darker needs. And they were not disappointed.

James ministered to them, as they were confident he would. His words were comforting, illuminating, and even inspiring—a balm for weary souls. Small wonder those Cambridge teachers kept coming back for more!

What James said about the contribution of psychology to teachers applies equally well to other subjects they are required to study. We who work with teachers instruct them in our various disciplines in the hope of awakening interests, broadening perspectives, strengthening convictions, even "fructifying independence" as James himself promised to do. In short, we teach what we do for a host of reasons, about which we usually are no clearer in our own minds than William James was in his. Our hopes, like his, are muddled much of the time.

"But wait a minute," calls out someone who is a teacher but not involved in teacher education. "How does the situation you describe differ from that facing teachers everywhere?"

"It doesn't," is the answer. Ask almost any teacher of almost any subject what he or she expects students to get out of that subject and the answer must surely resemble the one given here—provided, of course, he or she has engaged sufficiently in "a searching of the heart," as the teachers of James's day were said to do. How do they know that the body of knowledge they call history or mathematics or literature will have any of its hoped-for payoff in the lives of their students? Obviously, they can never know for sure. What we *do* know about the retention of what is learned in school is, alas, not very encouraging. Research tells us that the bulk of it disappears from memory almost before the ink on the pupil's report card is dry.

Yet some of it obviously endures. And even the portion that is forgotten leaves a residue of some sort that has a way of changing the person in whose mind it was temporarily housed. These changes are often unanticipated and seldom fully fathomed by the person experiencing them. But they are real nonetheless, we need have no doubt of that.

So, like teachers everywhere, what can we who work with teachers do beside face our classes with all the courage and hope we can muster? We can, of course, continue to probe the mystery of what happens when teachers and students meet, and well we should. We can, in that probing, turn to others, such as William James, to assist us in sorting out our own thoughts. But we must not expect easy answers, as the example of James's *Talks to Teachers* warns. Nor must we be unnerved should we encounter pockets of fog along the way, even when being shepherded by the best of guides.

Finally, how shall we come to terms with William James's thinly veiled contempt for teachers and those who teach them? Shall we be charitable and forgive him for it? I recommend we do. After all, he willingly accepted the invitation to talk to us, which is more than some of his colleagues would probably have done. His prejudice toward teachers of the elementary grades does seem to have blinded him to some of the complexities those teachers face in their class-rooms. More's the pity for that.

But even with hobbled insight, James spoke more sensibly and more eloquently to an audience of classroom teachers than many who are speaking today. He at least understood that teaching can never be reduced to a formula, an insight that seems to have escaped all too many of those who today continue to "lay the law down to teachers from above." He also had a way with words that today's platform speakers at educational conventions and teachers' institutes would do well to study carefully.

So let's let bygones be bygones and, instead of keeping our hands in our laps as some may feel inclined to do, let's join in the applause and the shouting that must have greeted Harvard's pride as he gathered up his notes and turned from the podium for the last time.

"Bravo, William James! Bravo and farewell!" Rest easy with your private thoughts and your sugared tongue. Listen to that ovation! Look at the smiles on the faces of the audience as they depart the hall! See how proud and straight those shoulders are beneath their frock-coats and shawls?

"You did it, Billy boy! You really pulled it off! Rest easy, friend of teachers. You old mystifier, you!"

3 THE UNCERTAINTIES OF TEACHING

"A TEACHER AFFECTS ETERNITY," Henry Adams once wrote, "He can never tell where his influence stops."[1] That brief statement, a mere twenty syllables in all, must surely come close to being the perfect tribute to the teaching profession. For what nobler sentiment could there be than the one expressed in its first four words—"A teacher affects eternity"!—and what truer observation than that contained in the remaining eight? "He can never tell where his influence stops." Inspirational, accurate, concise. A combination hard to beat. Small wonder, then, that Adams's famous pat on the back to teachers, penned more than seventy years ago, retains its appeal to this day.

Yet however fine those twelve well-chosen words may be for chiseling into the granite portals of schools or onto the headstones of dear departed teachers, they leave much to be desired when read as commentary on the really troublesome uncertainties connected with the act of teaching. Adams never meant them to be read that way, of course. He obviously was more intent on paying respect to teachers than on being either descriptive or analytic about the details of their work.

But questions about the more mundane and worrisome aspects of the ignorance from which teachers sometimes suffer are not long in surfacing once we have been stirred to think about the more inspirational aspects of their work. After wondering for only a few seconds about the farthest reach of a teacher's influence, I find my own thoughts pulled back to more mundane matters, almost as if by gravity. "What about the minute-by-minute influence teachers have on the pupils seated before their very eyes?" I ask myself, "How much do they know about what's going on in the here-and-now, an arm's length or so away?"

---

[1] *The Education of Henry Adams.* (Boston: Houghton Mifflin Co., 1918), 300.

"Much less than they probably would like to know," comes back my own answer to that question. For what teacher has not frequently wondered whether this or that student really understood a particular point or whether the class as a whole was following the line of an argument or had grasped the moral of a tale? None that I know of. And how many teachers are left wondering about such matters long after their students have gone home for the day and even after they are no longer their students at all? The bulk of them, I would wager. Indeed, I suspect that all teachers find themselves in such a quizzical mood from time to time.

So though we may concede that Adams was right about a teacher's influence extending forward *ad infinitum* and about his never knowing where that influence *stops*, in the interest of accuracy we must balance that noble thought with the rather more cynical observation that in all likelihood our poor teacher often cannot tell for sure where his influence *starts*! Doubtless there are as well times *between* start and finish when he also finds himself more puzzled than he would like about the impact he is having on his students.

These more mundane forms of uncertainty are often quite unsettling to teachers, far more so, as a rule, than are any of the unknowns having to do with their *long term* influence. It is easy to see why this is so.

As a teacher I may never live to discover that my efforts have altered the course of human history by so much as a hair's breadth, and if it turns out they have, it truly is a pity that I shall never learn of it. But if I characteristically go home *each day* doubting whether *anything* I did or said had *any* effect whatsoever on *anyone*, I am in a sorry state indeed, no matter what my future rewards might turn out to be.

The public as well might get around to thanking me and my teaching colleagues one of these days, as it belatedly realizes what a force for the good we've been. The mere prospect of such an acknowledgment is pleasant to contemplate. But if tomorrow the public at large begins to suspect that the students we teach are not learning what they are supposed to learn or are not changing in other ways that supposedly justify their going to school, we teachers throughout the land had better take cover.

So the dual considerations of how well teachers think they are doing and how well the public thinks the schools are doing are inextricably tied to the underlying question of what is being taken away by students from their school experience at the end of each school day. Uncertainty about the answer to *that* question can be and often is a source of genuine concern for teachers and for school people in general.

The possibility of teachers facing troubles of this degree of severity does not make them inevitable, of course. Some teachers may never encounter them at all. But the mere fact that we can easily *imagine* them tells us something about teaching that is worth pondering, something crucial to a full understanding of what the activity is all about.

A part of what it tells us has already been said: that teachers sometimes have a hard time proving their worth, even to themselves. Why this should be so is easy enough to understand. It derives in large measure from the fact that teaching, unlike masonry or brain surgery or auto mechanics or even garbage collecting, has no visible product, no concrete physical object to make or repair or call its own. Consequently, unlike workers in the forenamed and many other occupations, teachers suffer a distinct disadvantage. When their work is finished they have nothing tangible to show off as a fruit of their labor; no sturdy brick wall, no tumor-free brain, no smoothly purring engine, not even a clean back alley to point to with pride as evidence of a job well done.

Indeed, the very question of when the teacher's job is done, forget whether well or poorly, is problematic much of the time; it must be established by agreeing in advance upon some fairly arbitrary cutoff point, a time to call it quits, such as a date on the calendar or a set number of instructional sessions. Moreover, what is true of the termination of instruction is equally true of intervals along the way. Even the decision to end a single lesson is more often determined by the clock on the wall than by any judgment of pedagogical accomplishment.

Teachers are by no means alone in this regard, as should also be obvious. Consider, for example, the plight of ministers, priests, rabbis, therapists, performing artists, ambassadors of good will of all varieties—from office receptionists to public relations specialists—not to mention countless other workers whose chief concern is with how some special group of people think and feel about things. All lack a tangible product whose gradual transformation yields a clear-cut sign of progress. At the close of the day this large segment of our work force (teachers prominent among them) trudges home, figuratively speaking, empty-handed.

Just as we cannot say that teachers are alone in this regard, neither can we say that they are more discomforted by it than are others. Perhaps the reverse is true. Maybe receptionists, for instance,

are much more pained by the lack of concrete evidence of their effectiveness than are teachers. At the same time, it does seem reasonable
to consider teachers apart from all others, if only because every
occupation so burdened quite likely experiences this state of affairs
somewhat differently and therefore might be expected to cope with it
differently as well.

This likelihood sets the stage for what follows, which is to consider in some detail one major class of uncertainties connected with
teaching—those having to do with the pupils' understanding or mastery of the material being taught. These are by no means the only
uncertainties teachers face. Others could as easily have been chosen
instead, as we shall presently see.

Moreover, because the circumstances of teaching and the characteristics of those who teach vary so from place to place and from time
to time, what turns out to be puzzling and problematic for one
teacher may not be so for another. What teachers of today look upon
as a major source of concern may have been taken for granted, perhaps never even examined, by teachers a few generations back.

Despite these variations, certain commonalities *do* exist in the
way teachers characteristically view their work. Among the latter is a
perspective on teaching that is at once epistemological and psychological in outlook. Its epistemological slant derives from the fact that
teachers almost everywhere conceive their job, at least in part, as
having to do with the transmission of *knowledge* of one sort or another.

What this means in practice is that throughout their careers
teachers are constantly embroiled in the question of whether somebody actually *knows* something or other (as opposed to not knowing
it, merely appearing to know it, not having grounds for claiming to
know it, and such other formulations used to describe ignorance).
That question, as has been said, is epistemological in content and
psychological in orientation.

Yet it would be incorrect to describe teachers as caught up with
those questions in quite the way that either psychologists or epistemologists might be. For example, teachers are not typically concerned with the nature of knowledge *per se*. What distinguishes their
epistemological puzzlement is its focus on knowledge that is or is not
lodged, so to speak, in the minds of an identifiable (and usually
clearly identified) group of people known as their students. In other
words, when teaching is in progress one of the teacher's major worries takes the form of wondering *what is going on at this instant inside
the heads or minds of the person or persons being taught?* Do they under-

stand? Are they following me? Have they grasped the point? A parallel set of questions recur when instruction has ceased. *Did* they understand? *Did* they follow me? And so forth.

Questions such as these make manifest the psychological orientation of the teacher's perspective on his work. Broadly considered, his focus is epistemological, but his concern with each "bit" of knowledge is qualified by his worry about its location within the psyche of a specific person or group of people.

Nor can we describe the teacher's interest in such questions as academic, as we might those of a professional philosopher, let's say. The answers he gives to them have an important bearing not only on what his next pedagogical move will be but also on how well he thinks he has performed his work.

Teachers are not alone, of course, in raising questions of a nonacademic sort about what other people know or do not know. Almost everyone does so every day. Consider, for example, how many times each of us asks someone how to get somewhere or what the time of day might be.

There is a major difference, however, between the average questioner on the one hand, and teachers on the other: when the former asks whether a person does or does not know something, the forthcoming answer is not viewed as a partial function of what the questioner himself has done. The former, in other words, feels no personal responsibility for whether the knowledge is present and available or not.[2] Teachers, on the other hand, are not so situated. They are at least partially responsible for the answers to the questions they ask.

Another difference is that the knowledge most people inquire about during the course of day-to-day living is not of a "bookish" sort, whereas what interests most teachers decidedly is. The questions that come up in everyday affairs commonly deal with the here and now. They have to do with things like our plans for the day, how we feel about this or that, where we left the keys to the car, when our laundry will be ready, what time it is, and so forth. When the knowledge we are seeking *does* have a more abstract and generalizable quality—as when we ask someone for the dates of the Civil War or the formula for potassium nitrate—the exchange is properly de-

---

[2] An exception is when we are telling something to someone and pause to inquire whether he understands. But in such an instance the posture of the questioner is decidedly "teacherish" in nature.

scribed as "teacherly" in nature, even though neither of the participants would describe himself as either a teacher or a student.

Having said this much about a teacher's epistemological and
psychological orientation, we are ready to ask how he or she proceeds
to answer the many questions having to do with whether things are
going as anticipated. In short, how does he or she find out whether
students are learning what they should?

My own observations of teachers reveal four distinct strategies
for dispelling pedagogical uncertainty, at least insofar as it deals with
the substantive content of what is being taught. Not every teacher
may use them all, true enough, and the rare teacher who is only
indirectly answerable for what is being learned—such as a lecturer on
radio or television—may use none at all. Such exceptions aside, each
strategy strikes me as being common enough to be quickly recognized
by most teachers and probably by most laymen as well.

The first three occur while teaching is going on. The fourth takes
place before or after the fact, when teaching either is yet to begin or
has been brought to a halt, temporarily or permanently.

The least formal and the least intrusive of these four ways of
investigating what is happening in classrooms is the common one of
looking around the room for signs of students having difficulty with
what is being taught. This form of visual monitoring is most readily
observable when the teacher is delivering a lecture or conducting a
discussion, though it sometimes occurs during the supervision of
seatwork and study periods as well. What the teacher is looking for
on such occasions are spontaneous signs of understanding and interest or the lack thereof, the sort of thing communicated by the looks on
students' faces and their bodily postures. These would include nods
of assent, smiles, frowns, furrowed brows, raised eyebrows, head
scratching, fidgeting, droopy eyelids, and more, all of which speak
volumes about how we feel about things, whether we want them to
or not. Then there are all those less obvious clues, comprising what is
sometimes called "body language," whose meanings we often deci-
pher without being aware of doing so.[3]

---

[3]John Dewey, for one, clearly recognized the importance of the teacher's being
sensitive to these fleeting signs of student involvement in the lesson. As he put it, "The
teacher must be alive to all forms of bodily expression of mental condition—to puzzlement, boredom, mastery, the dawn of an idea, feigned attention, tendency to show
off, to dominate discussion because of egotism, etc.—as well as sensitive to the meaning of all expression in words. He must be aware not only of *their* meaning, but of their
meaning as indicative of the state of mind of the pupil, his degree of observation and
comprehension." (Dewey, *How We Think* [Lexington, Mass: D.C. Heath and Company,
1933], 275.)

A colloquial way of talking about what is going on during this kind of visual search is to say that when they behave in this way teachers are trying to find out whether or not the students are *with* them or whether they are *following them* in their understanding. If the students are not, they are sometimes spoken of as being *lost* or *out of it*, a condition that calls for some kind of remedial action.

The reciprocal nature of this process is worth noting in passing. Though the primary purpose of the teacher's visual scan is to seek information about the extent of the students' understanding of what is being taught, the scan is functional in its own right. It serves as a warning signal, reminding students to remain attentive and alert. Thus, by simply looking about, the teacher creates the conditions for the realization of what is sometimes called a self-fulfilling prophecy.

The second strategy for finding out how well students understand the material being taught is not nearly as observable as the one just described, though it is every bit as common. The reason it can't be observed as easily as are smiles and frowns is that it has more to do with "classroom atmosphere," which takes quite awhile to establish, than with anything the teacher says and does within any single teaching session. The kind of "atmosphere" being referred to is one in which students feel comfortable admitting ignorance, letting their teacher and fellow students know that they do not know or cannot do something. How is such an atmosphere established? By invitation, to start with. By inviting students to raise their hands or come up to the teacher's desk when they are having difficulty. But the sincerity of that invitation requires treating all such revelations with sympathy and understanding. Only in this fashion do students come to know that it is safe *not* to know. Only then can they be expected to reveal their ignorance willingly.

Because the raising of hands to seek aid from the teacher has become such customary behavior in most classrooms, the formality of announcing it as a rule to be followed is often unnecessary. (On the contrary, calls for help in the form of raised hands come so thick and fast in many classrooms that the teacher is obliged to slow them up or stop them completely by requesting that questions be held until the end of class or until a natural break occurs in the session.) But whether formally announced or not, this second strategy to determine how students are coming along with their lessons is fully as commonsensical as the first. It consists of nothing more complicated or unusual than seeing to it that students know they are welcome to call for help when they are in trouble.

A third commonplace technique for finding out whether students understand what is being taught is to ask them directly while teaching is underway. This type of questioning takes many forms, which vary chiefly in how precise they are, both with respect to the content of the question and the identification of the person or persons being asked.

At one extreme are very general queries addressed to no one in particular. These are often one-word questions, such as "Understand?" or "OK?" or "Right?" They usually call for little more than a nod of the head in reply. (Some teachers use this technique of questioning so habitually that they become hardly aware of doing so. I have witnessed more than one such teacher query his students with an "OK?" or "Get it?" while he himself was writing on the blackboard with his back turned to the class. Several students nodded in response to each question, but their nods went unseen by the teacher who continued to face the board as he moved ahead with his exposition of the material to be learned.)

At the other extreme, and much more interesting from a pedagogical point of view, are very specific questions addressed to particular students. Typically, the student being questioned is called upon to recite what he or she has learned about something or to demonstrate mastery of a skill by actually performing it. Pointed questions such as these usually cannot be ignored or "ducked" as can the more vague and general queries at the other end of the continuum. Thus, if the student does not know the answer or cannot perform as requested, he or she has no alternative but to reveal his or her ignorance to the teacher and, when the questioning is done in public, to fellow students as well.

The fourth procedure for seeking to find out what students have learned is the most formal of all. It occurs *outside* the instructional session itself, as has already been said, and entails the administration of tests, quizzes, exams, and a host of related activities. In addition to ordinary written tests, these include term papers, oral examinations, project reports, recitals, and a variety of other means of allowing or, more commonly, requiring students to display their newly acquired knowledge and skills. Because these procedures typically occur *after* a series of regular lessons, there ordinarily is an air of finality about them that is lacking in the three less formal methods that have been described.

Here, then, are four methods teachers commonly use to accomplish the complicated business of ascertaining what *is* going on or what *has* gone on in the heads or minds of their students. There may be other ways equally common, but I am unfamiliar with them. These, then, comprise what I look upon as a quartet of "classic" strategies by which teachers seek to reduce the uncertainties they face, at least insofar as those uncertainties have to do with what students know or do not know. To repeat, the four are:

1. Observing students in search of visual and auditory signs of involvement.
2. Arranging for the admission of self-perceived difficulties.
3. On-the-spot questioning for evidence of understanding.
4. Examining for the acquisition and retention of knowledge and skill after instruction has ceased or during intervals when it has been temporarily suspended.

How successful these procedures turn out to be will depend, of course, on the skill and consistency with which each is employed. Some teachers are no doubt better than others in using them. Some teaching situations, in all probability, lend themselves more easily to their applications than do others. Each may help to reduce the teacher's uncertainty somewhat, but none will eliminate it completely. It is relatively easy to see why this might be so.

To start with, it is widely known that the outward signs of inner attentiveness and understanding can be faked. Thus the teacher who relies solely on looking around to determine who is following what is going on might be in for a big surprise if he or she were to employ more stringent standards for gauging that understanding. In all fairness, however, it also must be said that the same teacher may also have a pleasant surprise or two in store as well. The student who appeared to be dozing off in the far corner of the room may miraculously turn out to have been the most attentive of them all. Successfully faked attentiveness and mistaken inattentiveness thus become the two most common sources of error when applying the first and most effortless of the four methods that have been mentioned.

The practice of relying on students to signal their own difficulties has drawbacks of its own, no less obvious than what the teacher can see with his or her own eyes. Teachers may do everything in their power to create an atmosphere in which students feel free to speak their minds and confess to troubles as they arise; however, not everyone, even in the most nonthreatening environment, is willing or able to take advantage of such an opportunity. Consequently, no matter how much the teacher might encourage students to speak up on such matters, there will always remain the nagging suspicion that some students are having difficulties but are not saying so.

As we turn from these two more or less passive strategies to the two more active ones—those involving questions the teacher puts directly to one or more students—we find their fallibility as methods to be somewhat different from those already mentioned, but no less troublesome. For example, those broad questions directed to the class as a whole through questions like "Understand?" or "Is that clear?" are so easy to answer falsely or to avoid answering at all that little more need be said about the potential inaccuracy of the information they provide. It is worth noting, however, that the answers given can be false in two ways. The student who nods his head when his teacher asks, "Understand?" may himself know that he doesn't *really* understand, but wishes to hide that fact from the teacher. However, it may also be the case that he *thinks* he understands (and therefore nods affirmatively) but actually does not. In both instances the student claims to know something he truly does not know, but in the first he is aware of his ignorance and in the second he is not.

On-the-spot questions with content, directed at particular students, may not leave the teacher guessing quite as much as do the more casual methods, but they are by no means error-free. If they are poorly worded, for example, the information they yield about a student's knowledge will be correspondingly ambiguous and hard to interpret. Moreover, once a question has been asked and answered in front of the rest of the students, its pedagogical usefulness is greatly diminished, if not fully spent. Teachers can and do follow up successful answers with queries like, "How many agree with Sarah?" but the reliability of the information received in reply is generally not much greater than when the teacher asks something like "Understand?"

As we move from the kind of questioning that goes on in class to the questions found in written tests, the same limitations apply as do those curtailing the usefulness of poorly worded on-the-spot questions. Although test questions are reusable in a way that in-class questions are not, that condition typically holds only if they remain a secret prior to the administration of the test. Once it is known that a specific question will be asked, its information yield is greatly diminished. This is so because most tests obviously do not include all the questions that could be asked about the subject at hand. Instead, they are a sampling, and sometimes not a very good one at that, from a larger pool of potential questions. Chiefly for this reason, they must remain confidential if the information they yield is to be of much use.

So much, then, for what seem to be some of the major sources of error in the standard procedures by which teachers try to find out how well students are dealing with the material being taught. There are, however, two additional costs that help to explain why teachers frequently pass over the more formal procedures in favor of the less formal ones. One has to do chiefly with the economics and the day-to-day usefulness of the information, the other with the socially intrusive nature of pedagogical questioning.

The initial set of considerations can be easily and quickly dealt with. What gives them substance, most of all, is the rather obvious fact that on-the-spot questions and formal tests are costly. Both take time that presumably could be spent on instruction. Moreover, if they are made and scored by the teacher himself, we must add additional hours to the cost of their use.

Then there is the discouraging fact that the information provided by tests usually arrives too late to be of much help in making instructional decisions. By the time most tests are given it is too late to go back and do much in the way of remedial work. Thus, the cost factor plus the practical usefulness of the information obtained take us a long way toward understanding why quizzes, exams, and other evaluative devices are not used more widely and frequently than they are.

"The socially intrusive nature of pedagogical questioning" is a phrase intended to cover many different aspects of the questions teachers ask, along with what is gained or lost by their asking. Strictly speaking, not everything labeled "intrusive" is deserving of that term, but each does "intrude," in a manner of speaking, by introducing a foreign element of sorts into what is otherwise one of the most common of all verbal interchanges—questioning and answering. The special character of the questions teachers ask transforms a common social exchange into one that is clearly out of the ordinary and, under certain circumstances, downright odd.

The *genuinely* intrusive nature of pedagogical questioning is grounded in the fact that each such question is a threat. The average student, as we all know, does not relish taking tests. More than that, many students genuinely fear them. Why so? Because of the risks involved. For the student whose answers turn out to be incorrect, the consequences can be very unpleasant indeed.

But what such students fear is deeper and more profound than the revelation of ignorance *per se*. To see that this is so, we need but ponder an ordinary situation in which a person is forced to confess a lack of knowledge. Consider, for example, what happens when someone is asked the time of day and does not have a watch, or is asked how to reach a certain destination and does not know the way. In such a circumstance, most persons would not be bothered at all by confessing their ignorance. They would simply say they didn't know and that would be that.

Not so in classrooms, however. There, faces redden and speech falters when a student is forced to admit that he or she doesn't know something. The reason for that difference, as we all know, is that students are *expected* to know the answers to the questions they have been asked, for the simple reason that such is what teaching is all about.

Thus, the first thing to keep in mind is that there are good reasons for at least some students wanting to avoid not only formal tests and final exams but also the teacher's direct questions when class is in session. Teachers know this, of course, and consequently are often reluctant to trigger the social tension that targeted questions or the announcement of an upcoming test introduce into their dealings with students. To keep their classes comfortable and relaxed, some teachers might go so far as to avoid all such procedures entirely.

As most teachers discover during the course of their careers, there are ways of taking most of the sting out of questioning. For example, one procedure for keeping "wrong" answers to a minimum is to address questions to the class as a whole, inviting only those who think they know the answer to speak up. This avoids much of the embarrassment created by calling on someone who must then admit ignorance, but it is by no means a foolproof way to avoid that embarrassment.

For one thing, not all volunteers are as smart as they think they are. Some turn out not to know the answers they seek to give. A few may even *know* they do not know, yet go on raising their hands on the chance that they won't be called upon anyway. But leaving aside the possibility of all such false information, the technique leaves the teacher in the dark with respect to all those students who do *not* volunteer. "Is it because they *don't* know the material," the teacher well may ask, "or are they simply reluctant to display their knowledge?"

Another way of keeping questions relatively unthreatening is to introduce humor into the situation, treating a wrong answer or the confession of ignorance as the occasion for some lighthearted remark designed to soften the blow. Still another technique is to applaud students for trying, even if they come up with the wrong answer. Experienced teachers doubtless could add to these examples until we had compiled a long list of ways to reduce the pain of testing. But no matter how many might be mentioned it is doubtful that all of them combined would be enough to remove all the sting from tests and direct questions. Such a list would, however, stand as an impressive acknowledgment of how real that sting truly is.

The only sure way of avoiding the potential discomfort associated with teachers' questions is not to raise them to start with. In some teaching situations this may be accomplished by sticking with the first two procedures—visual monitoring and the inviting of questions from students themselves—while foregoing all targeted queries from the teacher. This works best where the teacher/pupil relationship is quite informal and of brief duration, as, for example, in a public lecture. The speakers at such affairs, most of whom may properly be thought of as teachers, may occasionally wonder how much their audience has actually gained from what was said, but they seldom bother to ask. And for very good reason, of course. They might quickly lose their audience if they did! In most classroom situations, however, it is difficult to avoid direct questioning completely if the teacher, and sometimes the public as well, is not to be burdened by an intolerable amount of uncertainty.

Teachers' questions also differ from ordinary queries in that teachers usually know the answers in advance. What they do *not* know is whether their *students* know the answers. When most people ask questions they do so because they genuinely lack the information being sought. They seek it, in other words, *for its own sake*, and not for what it tells them about some more remote or secondary condition. There are obvious exceptions to this generalization, as a moment's reflection quickly attests. Sometimes, people ask questions just to be polite—e.g. "How are you?"—without being genuinely interested in the answer. They also at times ask questions rhetorically, without expecting any answer at all. Such exceptions notwithstanding, the generalization that most questions are asked for the sake of the answer given still holds.

Thus it is that whenever we have reason to suspect that a person asking a question already possesses the information being sought, we are naturally inclined to wonder about the motive behind the request. "If he already knows, why is he bothering to ask?" is the bluntest way of putting it. That question is a natural one to raise in most such situations.

The exception, as has been said, is when the questioner is a teacher. Teachers commonly ask questions whose answers they already know. They do so because they do *not* know whether the student being questioned can answer correctly. In other words, the teacher's real interest, in most instances, is in *the student's mastery* of the knowledge or skill in question, rather than the content of the answer *per se*.

This motive behind teachers' questions is no big secret to most people. Save for the very beginners in our schools—those in kindergarten or thereabouts—most students know full well that when a teacher asks a question it usually is to find out whether they (the students) know or can do something; it is not a search for an answer unknown to the teacher. Teachers themselves seldom go out of their way to disguise this fact.

At the same time, though it may be necessary for teachers to ask the questions they do, there remains something unnatural about their customary way of doing so. Unlike most questioners, teachers could as easily give the answer to the question as ask it. Everyone (save the very youngest students) may well understand that such a situation holds in most classrooms, but that understanding is usually insufficient to totally dispel the lingering suspicion that teachers are somehow less sincere, at least when it comes to asking questions, than are most other people.

Moreover, it is not just that teachers typically know the answers to the questions they ask which gives rise to the suspicion of their being insincere in the asking. There are deeper reasons for the mistrust that is often occasioned in such circumstances. To see why this is so we need consider two features of the conditions under which teachers typically ask questions.

The first of these features has to do with how close questioning follows on the heels of instruction. The second has to do with a common habit among teachers, which is to press on with their questioning after having been assured by their students that understanding has been achieved or that learning has taken place. Both such practices are perfectly understandable when we consider teaching as a total enterprise, but they do contribute to the mistrust already spoken of, all the same. To see why this might be so, consider the possible reasoning behind the teacher's actions. If a teacher has just taught something, what would make him wonder if students had learned it? And if students have already *told* their teacher that they have learned something, why would he or she then proceed to question their word?

The answer to the first of those two questions is much easier to give than is the answer to the second. The simple truth is that there are countless ways in which teaching might possibly go awry. All manner of mishap may account for something having gone wrong between the teacher's *delivery* of some piece of knowledge (or his recommendation that it be obtained from somewhere else such as a textbook), and its safe deposit in the student's memory bank or neurological network (or however one wishes to speak of its resting place within the person).

The student may not have heard what was said or seen what was done. He may have received the message but failed to comprehend its meaning. He may have understood perfectly a short while back but have now forgotten what he once knew. He may simply have failed to read the assignment and thus never come upon the knowledge in the first place. The possibilities go on and on. Thus, there are all kinds of reasons for a teacher to be curious about how successful his or her teaching has been as well as to check up on whether students have completed the work assigned them.

But let's say that such a query has been made and the student being questioned assures the teacher that he or she understands the material or has successfully completed the requisite assignment. Why should the teacher not take the student's word for it? Why press the matter further? The answers to those questions are also obvious to anyone who has been either a teacher or a student, which is to say almost everyone, but the fact that such pedagogical probes are understandable does not dissipate the air of distrust that often accompanies them. To see why this is so, consider the following hypothetical situation.

Suppose a gift of china is sent as a wedding present to the home of a prospective bride. A few days later the gift-giver calls the home of the bride-to-be to see if the gift arrived safely. "Yes it did," is the answer received. "I'd like to see for myself," the caller replies, "I'll drop by this evening if it's convenient."

What's strange about that situation? The obvious answer is: gift-givers don't usually insist on seeing that their gift has arrived safely once the recipient has assured them it has. To do so is to say, in effect, "I don't trust what you have told me. I must see for myself." Such a lack of trust is almost bound to be insulting, no matter how justifiable the gift-giver's worries about the safe receipt of the item that had been sent.

Though teachers are not exactly gift-givers, at least not like the one described, a close parallel with the social dynamics of that description occurs whenever a teacher begins by asking a student if he or she understands something and then proceeds to insist on the display of that understanding. "Did the knowledge arrive?" asks the teacher. "Yes," nods the student. "Let me see," says the teacher.

"What's the matter, don't you believe me?" the student inquires. "Sure I do," the teacher replies, "it's just that . . . ."

That what? The answer, I fear, is that a nugget of distrust *does* lie at the bottom of the teacher's demand for hard evidence of the student's knowledge, whether or not he or she wants to acknowledge it. Moreover, though we might wish it were otherwise, that distrust often turns out to be justified. Like it or not, people might have several good reasons to hide the fact that they do not know something, even people who are usually honest about most other things.

For one thing, an admission of ignorance is just plain embarrassing in many social situations. This is especially true when the knowledge in question is taken to be a mark of social status or prestige. For another, it reveals a deficit whose correction may be insisted upon. To admit we do not know something is to present ourself as a candidate for teaching.

Both of these consequences of admitting ignorance are heightened within classrooms. There the revelation of ignorance is particularly discomforting, especially when it follows on the heels of direct instruction. The student who confesses to not knowing what the teacher or the textbook has just finished teaching has obviously failed at what is clearly the central mission of the teaching enterprise. That failure may or may not be excusable. Perhaps the student failed to listen attentively, perhaps she failed to read the assignment, perhaps the teacher did *his* job poorly, but no matter what the explanation it remains a failure all the same.

Thus it is not very surprising to find that many students will not voluntarily reveal their ignorance about academic matters and will sometimes seek to keep it hidden even under direct questioning. So the suspicions underlying the teacher's mode of questioning are by no means unwarranted. Indeed, they are completely reasonable in the light of what we know about human nature. But the legitimacy of the teacher's suspicions does not make the act of putting them to rest any easier for either party. It is awkward, to say the least, to have to check up on people. And it is demeaning, if not downright insulting, to have to be checked up on. Legitimate they may be, but suspicions they remain.

Much has been said so far about the social and personal discomfort that can and often does surround the teacher's use of direct questions and tests, but this is not intended as an argument in favor of abandoning those practices in classrooms. On the contrary, if teachers are to fulfill their professional responsibilities they often have no choice but to insist that students display their newly acquired knowledge, or lack thereof, no matter how painful or embarrassing such a disclosure may be.

Although we acknowledge the necessity of teachers' questions, we can simultaneously begin to understand why we might find them used less frequently in practice than pedagogical theory might seem to dictate. In other words, we can start to see why many teachers might prefer to live with the uncertainty of not knowing for sure whether their students have in fact learned what was taught, even though all they have to do to find out is ask. The cost of obtaining that information must be weighed not only against its potential discomfort to individual students but also against the strain it puts on the social relationships within the classroom as a whole. We may condemn the teacher who avoids such discomfort at all costs, just as we might condemn the parent who never disciplines his or her child, but in both cases we can at least understand the motives behind their reluctance to act.

Up to this point our exposition of the uncertainties teachers face and their methods of coping with them has stayed within the embrace of a very familiar, if not uniformly popular, way of looking at the teacher's job. To give it a label, we will call the perspective taken thus far the "knowledge reproduction" point of view.[4] More metaphorically, the same perspective might be dubbed something like "the warehouse conception of school learning."

Essentially this view treats knowledge as a commodity of one kind or another that is deposited within a student's mind (or nervous system, if you prefer), where it remains, save for the ravages of memory loss and cerebral accidents, until it is called forth by the student or retrieved on command by some outside source. The essential point is that the stored knowledge is expected to retain its original shape, whether for inspection or use. In these terms the teacher's uncertainty about his or her success as a transmitter of knowledge

---

[4]This is not to be confused with the phrase "knowledge reproduction" as it appears in recent neo-Marxist critiques of our educational system. See, for example, Pierre Bourdieu and Jean-Claude Passeron, *Reproduction in Education, Society, and Culture* (London: Sage Publications Ltd., 1977). In essence, the latter set of critics charges that our schools are being used to "reproduce" the current distribution of knowledge (and therefore ignorance) in our society, thereby perpetuating existing social class, ethnic, and racial divisions within the country at large. As the phrase is used here it is completely devoid of all such critical overtones and bears no relation whatsoever to the neo-Marxist argument.

boils down to whether the material he or she believes to have delivered (or ordered sent) has actually arrived safely and is currently in storage where it is readily retrievable by the students.

This uncertainty is commonly relieved simply by asking the student to show a receipt of some kind (a nod of understanding is often good enough) or, if need be, by asking that the goods be delivered for inspection (usually a sample will suffice). Much of teaching and much of testing conform to this model.

Although this way of looking at what teachers do has been severely criticized by educational reformers for centuries—usually on the grounds that it is too mechanical a model or because it places too much emphasis on rote memory—there can be no doubt, like it or not, that it does capture an important piece of truth about schooling. Only thus can we explain its endurance over the years.

But the recurrent criticism of this view by thoughtful educators makes it equally clear that the piece of truth it contains is not the whole cloth. Not all of schooling conforms to the "knowledge reproduction" model—perhaps not even the most important part at that. John Dewey, for example, had this to say about the inadequacies of the metaphors commonly employed to embody the "knowledge reproduction" point of view.

> It is hardly an exaggeration to say that too often the pupil is treated as if he were a phonograph record on which is impressed a set of words that are to be literally reproduced when the recitation or examination presses the proper lever. Or, varying the metaphor, the mind of the pupil is treated as if it were a cistern into which information is conducted by one set of pipes that mechanically pour it in, while the recitation is the pump that brings the material out again through another set of pipes. Then the skill of the teacher is rated by his or her ability in managing the two pipelines of flow inward and outward . . . . The mind is not a piece of blotting paper that absorbs and retains automatically. It is rather a living organism that has to search for its food, that selects and rejects according to its present conditions and needs, and that retains only what it digests and transmutes into part of the energy of its own being.[5]

To give a name to the "living organism" view that Dewey espoused, we will call it the "knowledge *transformation*" model, thus differentiating if from the "knowledge *reproduction*" point of view that

---

[5] John Dewey, *How We Think* (Lexington, Mass.: D.C. Heath and Company, 1933), 261-262.

has already been explicated. Its emphasis is upon the process whereby knowledge is assimilated or transformed or otherwise adapted to fit within the learner's system of habitual thought and action. Within the physical world the closest analogy to this epistemological transformation is obviously the one Dewey himself used—the physiological process of digestion.

What interests us within the present context is what such a shift of metaphors does to the uncertainties of teaching. The changes they undergo are radical indeed. Under the transformation model the teacher is no longer primarily concerned with whether some fragile commodity called knowledge has arrived safely and is properly stored somewhere in its original carton, so to speak. Rather, the central questions now have to do with such things as how the knowledge in question is being used by the learner, how it relates to what was learned before, how it becomes personalized by being translated into the learner's own language, how it becomes applied to new situations, and so forth. In cognitive terms the focus is no longer on the power of memory alone. It now encompasses levels of mental functioning that customarily fall under the rubrics of "judgment" and "understanding."

Something else happens when we change metaphors. Not only are the teacher's uncertainties more numerous and more complex than before, but they are of a different nature entirely. No longer can the knowledge-sent/knowledge-received comparison be judged by a standard that approximates the philosopher's correspondence theory of truth. In the reproduction model, it will be recalled, what is "withdrawn" from the student during questioning or testing is essentially the same, structurally speaking, as what was "deposited." Ideally, the two are identical. Under the transformation model, however, the before and the after, so to speak, no longer match up.

In other words, not only is the teacher uncertain whether or not his or her students will be capable of answering questions correctly; she or he is also no longer quite sure of what questions to ask. The teacher's total approach to the task must be more exploratory and open-ended. Under the transformation model the teacher is not only searching for answers, but searching for questions as well.

The greater complexity of the questioning process under the knowledge transformation model, plus the fact that it is more "organically" derived and therefore presumably more suited to human affairs, may make it seem decidedly superior to the knowledge reproduction point of view as an outlook to be adopted by teachers everywhere. Such has been the judgment of countless educational reformers, from Comenius forward. All have hailed some form of an educational model whose metaphors derive from life processes as a decided advance over earlier and more "mechanical" perspectives.[6]

But the real issue is not whether the knowledge transformation point of view is inherently superior to the knowledge reproduction outlook. Rather, it is: When is one or the other the most helpful way of thinking? For example, in foreign language teaching the knowledge reproduction view seems quite appropriate much of the time. The same may be true of many other subjects whose goal is to have students reproduce with precision what they have learned.

If, as seems true, certain subject matters may be better suited to the application of one model rather than the other, it would follow that teachers of different subjects will be faced with different degrees and kinds of uncertainty. It is also probable that whichever way of looking at the process is adopted, the business of conveying knowledge is sometimes treated more casually than at other times by both the teachers and students involved and by the public at large as well. In short, we worry more about whether some people are knowledgeable, in either a reproductive or a transformative sense, than we do others. For example, we seem to care more whether a physician "knows his stuff" than we do, say, about a florist. Consequently, we would expect teachers in a medical school to be somewhat more conscientious and demanding about asking questions and giving tests than we would teachers of floral design.

The overall level of such worries seems to change over time as well. Right now we appear to be in the middle of a period of heightened interest in the outcomes of schooling, particularly at the secondary level and below. Consequently, we hear a lot of talk these days about such notions as educational accountability and minimal competency testing. How long the present trend will continue remains to be seen. But so long as such a mood prevails teachers are bound to feel additional pressure upon them to seek "hard" evidence of what is or is not being learned by their students.

However and whenever both the knowledge reproduction and the knowledge transformation models are employed as tools of

---

[6]The urgent pleading for this change in root metaphors still goes on. Myron Atkin of Stanford University and Ernest House of the University of Illinois, for example, have recently called for a shift from "metaphors drawn from factory production" to "biological imagery" when thinking about educational change. See M. Atkin and E. house, "The federal role in curriculum development, 1950-1980," *Educational Evaluation and Policy Analysis* 3, Number 5 (September-October, 1981), 33.

thought, together with the assortment of metaphors that serve to make them concrete, they are limited in one and the same way. Both refer exclusively to the acquisition of knowledge as the proper end of education.

Naturally, no one would argue that knowledge should *not* be central to any conception of educational goals. That much can be granted at the start. But it is certainly reasonable to ask whether "knowledge," however defined, covers all that schooling and education are about. Historically, at least since ancient Greece, the answer to that question has been no.

For centuries schools have sought to do many other things above and beyond the passing along of knowledge, whether conceived of "mechanically" or "organically." They have tried to form character, to develop habits, to arouse interests, to change attitudes, to create values, and more. Knowledge of one kind or another may be an essential component of all such undertakings, but whether it is *all* that matters is a question that has concerned educators and philosophers for centuries.[7] Today's practicing educators—the handful of Mr. Gradgrinds among them set aside—seem unanimous in believing that there is a world of difference between the transmission of knowledge *per se* and the goal of developing character or arousing social consciousness or any of the other broad goals that have been historically associated with the mission of the schools.

This being so, the question now becomes: What happens to the uncertainties of teaching when we move to aims that are not strictly epistemological in character? What do we do to determine whether attitudes are really changing or appreciations developing or any of the other things happening that, as educators, we would so like to see?

Under such circumstances, are there questions to ask and tests to give? A few perhaps. In seeking to assess the development of a proper set of attitudes, for example, one can administer written tests in much the same manner as is done for factual knowledge. We must note, however, that the interpretation of the answers to such tests is considerably trickier than is true for straightforward tests of knowledge.

---

[7] Socrates, for one, claimed that virtue was knowledge, by which he meant that the only reason people did not behave virtuously was because they lacked proper knowledge concerning the consequences of their actions, or something of that sort. However, despite its historical significance, Socrates' argument remains less than totally convincing.

For the most part, however, the questioning procedures fitted to the epistemological goals of schooling cannot be adopted whole cloth to help teachers resolve those uncertainties that arise from efforts to attain other, quite different, educational ends. Indeed, it is entirely possible that some aspects of a teacher's influence are not to be revealed by *any* sort of question, not even by the most skillful teacher or test-maker.

There are even times, it seems, when the most sensible thing for a teacher to do at the end of a lesson is to remain silent and in so doing to make peace with whatever uncertainties he or she may have. Elizabeth Hardwick, teacher and author, describes one such occasion. "It's hard to say anything about a fine short story," she tells us. "I know from teaching that I would ask the class to read Chekhov and all I could think to say to them was, 'Isn't he wonderful!'" Most gifted teachers, I would warrant, have had similar moments of speechlessness.

On such rare yet glorious occasions the question of whether a tiny kernel of knowledge is or is not lodged in somebody's head seems trivial. So does much else. Sometimes when things are going their very best in classrooms questions of all sorts seem strangely out of place. At such moments our thoughts may well return with profit to Henry Adams and his famous saying about all the things teachers will never know. With each day of teaching that host of uncertainties confronts us anew.

Insofar as the farthest reach of a teacher's influence is concerned—the portion receding beyond the limits of human vision—Henry Adams in his famous quotation certainly hit the nail on the head. But, had he been content with a less lofty though more accurate observation, he could as easily have used the close at hand as a starting place. "Near and far," he might have said, "the limits of a teacher's influence remain forever obscure." Therein lies the fate of all who teach—from here to eternity, uncertainties galore.

4   REAL TEACHING

THERE USED TO BE A GAME SHOW on television some years back whose format was as simple and straightforward as it was entertaining. The show's panelists—four "TV personalities" as they are usually called—were introduced to successive trios of strangers, each made up of one person who worked at some unusual occupation, such as taming lions or cutting diamonds, plus two others of the same sex and supposedly the same name who claimed to be similarly employed but were actually imposters. The point of the game was to identify the honest member of each trio by asking all three of them questions about the line of work in which they claimed to be engaged. When the time limit for questions had been reached and each of the contestants had made a guess as to which of the three was telling the truth, the show's announcer would call upon the *real* Mister or Miss So-and-So to stand and be identified. Cries of surprise, followed by laughter and applause, crowned the departure of each trio of contestants.

That once popular show, called "To Tell the Truth," invariably comes to mind whenever my thoughts turn to the question of what teaching is like as an occupation and how it might be defined. It does so because the show's format reminds me of an experience I had some time ago as a newly appointed principal of a nursery school. That experience is itself worth describing in some detail, for it introduces in a rather dramatic if lighthearted way the questions to be examined in this chapter.

I was a newcomer to both school administration and nursery schools at the time. Consequently, in order to familiarize myself with the institution and how its teachers behaved I spent as much time as I could during my first few weeks on the job poking about the school as a complete stranger might, watching what was going on and trying to get a feel for the place. The teachers, who wanted to get to know me as much as I did them, warmly welcomed me to their classrooms. Their doing so made the experience as enjoyable as it was informative.

As the days wore on I slowly became aware of certain things the teachers did that distinguished them from the kinds of teachers I had spent most time with in the past—those with much older pupils. For example, I noticed that when nursery school teachers spoke to individual children or listened to what they had to say they first descended to the child's height by bending at the knees until their faces were on a level with the child's own. At the same time, I was bemused to note, when I myself spoke or listened to a child I tended to bend at the *waist* rather than the knees. As a result, I hovered above the tyke like some huge crane, causing him or her to gaze skyward and, if out of doors on a bright day, to shade the eyes while doing so.

I noticed also that when reading to pupils the nursery school teachers did something else both odd and amusing. They propped the books they were reading on their laps with the open pages facing the students. The reason for doing so was obviously to allow the children to see the book's illustrations. But what made such a natural thing so amusing to me was that it required the teachers to develop the knack of reading upside down!

These and other examples of what seemed to me to be characteristic behavior of nursery school teachers so intrigued me that I decided to share my discoveries with the teachers themselves. I thought it possible they might add to my store of examples. I also expected them to be mildly amused by my report on the outcome of my observations.

Broaching the topic over lunch one day, I rather casually announced that it seemed as though my observations around school were beginning to pay off. "I think I'm beginning to catch on to a few of the tricks of your trade," I began. "For example, I've noticed that when you teachers . . ." and then I described a few of the things I had seen, mimicking postures and gestures in a somewhat exaggerated way, just to add to the fun. I concluded by claiming that should the chance ever occur to pass myself off as a nursery school teacher, I now thought I knew enough to be easiy mistaken for the real McCoy.

My mimicking of their behavior amused the teachers, as I had thought it would, and so did my boast at the end. But the latter, rather surprisingly, turned out to be more than simply amusing. It triggered a discussion that went on far past lunch, one that we returned to on several occasions in the ensuing months. The focus of that recurrent discussion was whether I or anyone else could indeed get away with impersonating a teacher without ever being found out and what it would mean, insofar as teaching is concerned, if that were to happen.

The teachers could easily imagine a person getting away with such a pretense for quite some time. They even conceded that I might succeed in doing it myself for a while. But the notion of someone pretending to be a nursery school teacher and *never* getting caught, was a condition they found puzzling. For if the person were never found out, they reasoned, shouldn't we at some point stop thinking of him or her as an imposter, even though this knowledge remains his or her own secret? Indeed, should the 'teacher' not at some point stop thinking of himself or herself that way? In short, when does the successful imposter actually become the real McCoy, or does that never happen? If not, why not?

A closely related question that we also discussed was whether the imposter had only to *behave* like a nursery school teacher in order to carry off the deception or whether there was more to it than that. Some of the teachers thought it would be necessary for the imposter to *think* like a nursery school teacher in order to *behave* like one. But that introduced the question of what it meant to think like a teacher. How does a nursery school teacher think?

The teachers and I went round and round in our discussions of these and other questions about teaching, all stimulated by my casual and, as I thought at the time, humorous observation that it might be possible to get by as a nursery school teacher without any formal training whatsoever. From that starting point, we soon discovered, the paths of speculation fan out in many directions. Can one determine whether a teacher is genuine or a fake (or good rather than bad) simply by watching her or him? Can teaching be defined behaviorally? What does it mean to say that teaching in general or good teaching in particular can be defined in any way at all? Where might such a definition come from? Is it something discovered or decided upon? If the former, how is that accomplished? If the latter, who does the deciding? And so on.

As could be guessed, the teachers and I never did succeed in answering most of the questions we so enthusiastically and, I fear, naively wrestled with back then. Nor have I yet done so. But both individually and collectively we did develop some tentative notions about the directions in which a few of the answers might lie. For me at least, several of those tentative notions have since become convictions.

What are they? Insofar as they relate to the topic of this chapter, my convictions are three in number. The first says there is no such thing as a behavioral definition of teaching and there never can be. We can never simply watch a person in action and be sure that something called teaching is going on. The second, closely related to the first, says that our attempt to say when a person is or is not teaching is always an act of interpretation. We are forever "readers" of human action, seeking to determine which "reading" is correct from among those possible. The third conviction, one that follows on the heels of the first two, denies the possibility of our ever arriving upon an enduring definition of what it means to teach. In the remainder of this chapter each of those propositions will be treated in turn.

I.

To begin, let's return to my early days as a nursery school principal, wandering from class to class in order to learn what nursery school teaching was all about. Picture my going about that task. Do you imagine I was very puzzled about when a teacher was or was not teaching? I assure you I was not.

As I moved from one room to another I *saw* with my own eyes teachers teaching and I did not for a moment doubt my judgment. Teaching was what I was witnessing, no doubt about it. One would have had to have been blind not to see it.

"But hold on now," as my conversations with the nursery school teachers later forced me to say to myself. "Is the observation of teaching really as simple and straightforward as that? What made me so confident that what I was witnessing every step of the way was something called teaching?"

Before answering those questions I must distinguish between two uses of the word "teaching." One treats it as an enterprise, the other as an activity.[1] When we speak of a person holding a job as a teacher we might describe him or her as now teaching in such-and-such a school or in such-and-such a city even though we know perfectly well that the person being talked about is at this moment home in bed (assuming it to be very late at night), or outside playing golf (if a Sunday afternoon). In other circumstances, however, when we say so-and-so is teaching, what we mean is that he or she is doing so at this very moment. In the first instance teaching is being treated as an enterprise, in the latter, an activity.

The former use of the term is obviously inclusive of the latter, for

---

[1]The distinction is more fully explicated in Paul Komisar's "Teaching: act and enterprise," C.J.B. Macmillan and Thomas W. Nelson (editors), *Concepts of Teaching: Philosophical Essays* (Chicago: Rand McNally, 1968), 63–88.

one would never describe a person as engaged in teaching as an enterprise if it were never true that he or she engaged in teaching as an activity. Nonetheless, the distinction is a useful one to keep in mind all the same.

Returning now to my feeling of confidence as I observed the nursery school teachers in action, we may ask again how I knew that what I was seeing were instances of teaching. Should someone have asked me that question at the time, I think I would have answered somewhat as follows:

> "Well, to start with, I know this is a school I'm in, right? I know these are classrooms and I know the adults in these classrooms are either teachers or teachers' aids. (I also happen to know which are which.) I watch what the teachers are doing and I see that their doings are episodic in nature, which is to say, they do one thing for a while and then they do something else. These episodes are units—atoms, if you like—of teaching behavior. Seeing them, recording them, describing them to others (as I did over lunch), are easy enough to do. There is nothing difficult or mysterious about the process at all."

Most people would probably give such a common sense explanation or something very much like it in a similar circumstance. The notion that teaching is what teachers can be seen doing seems sensible enough as an observational guide. There are limits to such a principle, of course, but everyone seems to know what they are. For example, if the teacher stops to tie his shoes or take off his jacket, or if he steps out in the hall for a drink of water, most people would not think of describing such actions as instances of teaching behavior. Thus it is tacitly assumed by most observers that not *everything* a teacher does while on the job is classifiable as teaching, though *most* of it probably will be. Many of the actions to be excluded are easily agreed upon.

A somewhat more difficult distinction is called for by the teacher who is standing in front of the class with his or her arms folded, waiting for the noise to abate. Is she or he at that instant teaching or merely getting ready to teach? And what about the teacher who is monitoring seatwork or marking papers? Should those activities be counted as part of teaching as well?

Judgments about such matters seem to depend, in part, on why the teacher in question is being observed in the first place. A supervisor of student teachers, for example, might find it very important to comment on the way a trainee prepared the class for instruction. From his or her point of view, standing in front of the class with arms folded is very much part of a teacher's repertoire of attention-getting devices and therefore is definitely an aspect of teaching worthy of comment.

Contrast that situation with someone doing research on teaching via an observational device focusing exclusively on teacher-pupil interaction. Under those circumstances, coding would begin when instruction was actually underway. Until then, from the researcher's point of view, teaching had not yet begun.

These examples point to a well-known truth, that some of a teacher's actions are easier to classify as instances of teaching than are others. When a teacher is explaining something to students or demonstrating a skill that is later to be imitated, who can doubt that at that instant teaching is underway? Similarly, when teachers are listening to students or watching what they do, there seems little or no ambiguity about whether or not they are actually teaching.

It is when the interactions between teachers and students do not obviously bear upon what is to be learned that the greatest uncertainty arises. But even these ambiguous instances are often resolvable once the observer's purposes are known. What aspects of a teacher's behavior are to be counted as instances of teaching is a question whose answer depends on prior considerations having to do with the circumstances under which the question is raised in the first place.

An additional distinction related to how to talk about teaching introduces an argument with an interesting history in education and in philosophy as well. It has to do with whether we should keep separate the idea of teaching as an accomplishment from that of teaching as an effort, an attempt to do something.[2]

One way of managing this dispute would be to limit the use of the term "teaching" to its sense as something that has been accomplished. This would require that we insist on evidence that learning has occurred before we can acknowledge that teaching has occurred.

---

[2]The distinction between words that describe our trying to do something and words covering our success in having done it was brought to the fore within philosophical circles by Gilbert Ryle in his influential book, *The Concept of Mind* (New York: Barnes and Noble, 1949). In that work Ryle distinguished between what he called "task verbs" and "achievement verbs." The former refer to things one is trying to do, the latter to things one has done. For example, "kicking" is a task verb, "scoring" an achievement verb. A similar distinction holds between treating and healing, hunting and finding, listening and hearing, and so forth. Teaching, as luck would have it, has come to be used in both senses, as something tried and as something accomplished, hence the confusion that plagues our understanding when it is not clear which of these senses applies.

John Dewey, for one, seems to have something like this in mind when he tells his readers that,

> Teaching may be compared to selling commodities. No one can sell unless someone else buys. We should ridicule a merchant who said that he had sold a great many of goods although no one had bought any. But perhaps there are teachers who think that they have done a good day's teaching irrespective of what pupils have learned. There is the same exact equation between teaching and learning that there is between selling and buying.[3]

Were we to take Dewey seriously on this point, it would affect the way we discussed what we saw when we observed teachers in action. The discovery that the students we had observed had learned nothing from their teacher would force us to acknowledge that the teacher had not been teaching, no matter what she might have appeared to be doing when we observed her. She may have been *trying* to teach, we might readily admit, but she wasn't actually teaching.

Under certain circumstances it makes good sense to restrict the use of the term in this way. It does so when it comes to what we would like to say about the activity, especially when we speak of teaching in the past tense. To say that Jones taught Smith how to swim but Smith learned nothing whatsoever about the sport does sound a bit peculiar, if not downright contradictory. It makes us want to counter with, "Well then, Jones didn't *really* teach Smith how to swim."

But note that if we insist upon this necessary connection between teaching and learning we then find it impossible to say with certainty that a person is teaching until after the fact—until evidence that learning has occurred is in hand. Lacking such evidence, all we can say as we watch teachers in action is that they *look* as though they are teaching, or perhaps, "They are definitely trying to teach." To put the matter somewhat differently, by too strict an insistence on the teaching-learning connection we automatically rule out the possibility of unsuccessful teaching.

To qualify as an instance of teaching, if a teacher's actions *must* result in learning, then we are left with the question of what to call the same set of actions when such a result is not forthcoming. They can't be called instances of teaching that didn't work, for we have just

---

[3]John Dewey, *How We Think* (Lexington, Mass.: D.C. Heath and Co., 1933) 34–35.

ruled out that possibility. Treating them as "tries," rather than "successes," allows us to declare that the teacher has tried to teach, which may be quite enough to say in many circumstances. Indeed, it could be that in everyday affairs that's what most people mean when they use the term. When we say, "Look, there's a person teaching," what we mean is, "There's a person trying to teach." The "trying to" is understood. Its omission is simply a kind of verbal shorthand.

To short-circuit an argument that seems to get more and more picayune as it goes along, most people would probably be content to have the phrase "trying to" tacked on to their descriptions of teachers in action wherever the word "teaching" appears. The cost of such a grammatical change seems a small price to pay for avoiding what could be an interminable debate. But note that by inserting such a qualifier in our speech we do not manage to sidestep the problem entirely. Indeed, we simply carry it with us. We may no longer face the question of how we know when a person is teaching, but we now must ask how we know when a person is *trying* to teach.

II.

We can answer that question with confidence, it would seem, in only one of two ways. Either we must have some prior knowledge of what trying to teach looks like, or we must trust the testimony of the person who says that is what he or she is doing. Let's look at the first possibility a little more carefully.

How did I know that the teachers I witnessed in the nursery school were trying to teach? Perhaps I possessed at the time some idea of what "trying to teach" looks like in general. The rest is simply a matter of matching the teachers observed with that prior conception. In other words, because those teachers were behaving in ways I recognized as being "teacherly," I confidently concluded that they were trying to teach. Is that the way my sense of recognition worked?

Something like that process must surely have been in operation, no doubt, but is it sufficient to explain my feeling of confidence? I think not. To understand why, consider the following situation.

A visitor to a school peeks through the window of a classroom door and sees a woman with chalk in hand standing before a group of approximately twenty-five young people seated at desks. The woman is gesturing toward a mathematical formula written on the blackboard. The visitor naturally concludes that he is witnessing a class in session; he is corrected by the principal, who happens by with the news that what is going on in that room is not a class at all but rather a rehearsal of a scene from the play, *The Prime of Miss Jean Brodie*, which the local drama society is putting on in a few days.

What does such an unlikely turn of events tell us about the problem of identifying an instance of someone trying to teach? Obviously, the observer who thinks he knows an act of teaching when he sees it can be fooled. People can pretend to teach. The whole scene can be make-believe. That rarely happens, of course, but it *could* happen and that's the important point. In other words, the identification of teaching can never be made on visual evidence alone. Something else is required, something having to do with the genuineness of the total situation.

Recall that when the hypothetical questioner asked why I was so confident in my judgment, I began by saying that I knew this was a school and these were classrooms and those people teachers and those students. I was confident, in other words, that I was not walking around a movie set, witnessing the filming of *Up the Down Staircase* or something like that.

There was even a touch of impatience in my answer, for my imaginary interrogator seemed to question the obvious. But my answer showed that my sense of confidence very much depended on a host of half-buried assumptions, beginning with the few I have mentioned and including many others as well.

Not only did I know what schools and classrooms and teachers were like, being able to recognize them on sight, and trusting my conviction that I was witnessing the real McCoy, but I also knew a reasonable amount about the ends those objects were designed to serve (or prepared to fulfill, as we would say of teachers themselves). I further knew something about their historical development, their political and social significance, and so on. In other words, the events I was witnessing were embedded within a cultural and historical context of which I was only partially conscious at the time, but one that infused them with meaning, all the same. That gave me confidence that I was witnessing an instance of teaching and not something else. Without that background of tacit understanding my feeling of confidence could never have arisen.

What I am saying here should remind us of the section of Chapter 1 that dealt with common sense and the role it plays in teaching. Here we seem to be saying that common sense (or "school sense," if that term is preferred) also plays an important role in our observations of teachers and in our talk about what they do. This extrapolation from what was said earlier should hardly come as a surprise, for there it was acknowledged that almost everything we do depends in large measure on common sense. But there is something additional being said here that is well worth highlighting.

The point to be noted is that teaching, like most other human actions, is not so much "seen" as it is "read." In other words, though we may feel that what we are witnessing in classrooms is as plain as the nose on our face (as I did during my wanderings about the nursery school), we feel that way thanks to the largely unconscious operation of a vast apparatus of understanding that we seldom bother to bring to the surface of awareness for close scrutiny.[4]

Here an illustration may help. Recall that I was impressed by the way the nursery school teachers lowered their whole upper torsos by bending at the knee when they wanted to speak to one of their pupils, whereas I bent over at the waist to achieve the same goal. The teachers' way seemed so much better than mine, so obviously superior as an adaptation to the difference in height between adult and child that I felt a little chagrined at not having thought of doing it that way myself. I "saw" immediately that it was a better way of doing things.

But was my sight as unaided by thought and reason as I felt it to be at the time? Did the superiority of the teachers' method require nothing but the naked eye to discern? Upon reflection, I realized that more than that was involved.

As a solution to the problem of how to move within speaking and hearing distance of a very small child, my way was just as good as the teachers', at least in physical terms. I could speak to the children and hear what they said just as well as they. What made their way superior was what the posture symbolized and what it might possibly communicate to the children.

Instead of the child having to crane his neck skyward, as he was forced to do when speaking to me, when his own teachers talked to him he was able to face them at eye level. That physical relationship was at once more intimate and less threatening than was my crane-like posture. It was also more egalitarian.

But why did I immediately see that as a better way of doing things? Who cares if a child has to crane her neck a little when talking to adults? Why should teachers worry about such things as creating an atmosphere of equality in the classroom?

The answers to such questions obviously call for more than meets the eye. They rest on assumptions built into my way of looking

---

[4] A process similar to the one described here is treated in some detail by Michael Polanyi in his book, *Personal Knowledge* (Chicago: University of Chicago Press, 1958). Polanyi referred to these unarticulated forms of knowing as "tacit knowledge."

at what I saw in those classrooms. Alter those assumptions and my perception of the events alters with them.

In other words, my response to what I saw was not nearly as automatic as I felt it to be at the time. What seemed blatant and obvious in the teachers' behavior was actually an interpretation of a fairly complicated sort. I not only saw what the teachers *did*, I also saw (or thought I saw) *why* they behaved as they did. In short, their actions made sense to me.

That sense was not a function of the stimulus properties of what I witnessed. Rather, it arose from prior understanding that I as an observer brought to the act of observing. Both the teachers and I knew the rules of the game, so to speak. That combination of tacit knowledge and *a priori* reasoning was what made possible my seemingly effortless "reading" of what appeared before my eyes in those nursery school classrooms.

This insight, which may not be much of a revelation to most people, is obviously not limited to what happens when we look at teachers. The same holds true when we observe anything in the world around us. In short, the meaning and significance of everything we see and hear is, in essence, an interpretation of the information provided by the senses.

Oddly enough, though the interpretative nature of our perceptual encounters with the world is clear enough when we pause to think about how we make sense of things, we tend to lose sight of it much of the time. We become so used to so many common sights and sounds that we no longer experience them as being in any way problematic. We know what they are and what they mean, just by looking at them—the way I looked and listened in those nursery school classrooms some years back. Once we are sufficiently familiar with an object or an event, its meaning becomes transparent, enabling us to short-circuit the initial phase of our puzzling encounter with what we now know. We forget, in other words, that meanings are achievements, partial creations rather than givens, and we also lose sight of the fact that they are vulnerable to change.[5]

It is well that our minds work this way most of the time, for if we had to ponder afresh each thing we saw and heard, life would be

---

[5] The notion that our conception of reality is a "construction" rather than a "given" plays a large part in the branch of social science known as "the sociology of knowledge." For an influential statement of recent thinking in this field see Peter L. Burger and Thomas Luchmann, *The Social Construction of Reality* (Garden City, N.Y.: Doubleday, 1966). The classic statement of this position is to be found in the essays of Karl Mannheim. See Paul Kecskemeti, (ed.) *Essays on the Sociology of Knowledge* (New York: Oxford University Press, 1952).

more of a puzzle than most of us could stand. At the same time, we also need to recognize the importance of questioning, now and again, our habitual way of interpreting the world. By so doing we make a wager in which there can be no loser.

Either such questioning will alter the way we see things, in a manner that is somehow more satisfying than our former view, or it will deepen our commitment to the interpretation we have already put upon reality. We stand to win either way. The task of looking at the familiar as if it were once again strange is far from easy. Some would call it impossible.[6] But the potential benefits more than repay the effort involved.

To relate this to teachers and teaching we need only acknowledge that teachers are no less caught up in the task of interpreting what goes on around them than are any of the rest of us. They too are faced with the unending chore of attaching meaning and significance to what they see and hear as they go about their work as teachers. That acknowledgement may sound innocent enough perhaps, but its consequences are considerable, not only for the way we look at teachers but also for the way they look at themselves.[7]

The observation that teachers are caught up in interpreting what goes on around them does not distinguish them from anyone else. Moreover, even when we consider the content of what they are called upon to interpret, we find an enormous overlap between the experience of teachers and that of the rest of us. As we have already noted, at the simplest level teachers need to know what chairs and tables and doors and countless other objects are for, just as the rest of us do. They must also recognize the significance of innumerable social actions—gestures, speech, and the like—as must we all. Given this shared interpretive obligation, we may wonder whether there is anything at all distinctive or unique about the way teachers view their surroundings. In short, is there anything like a pedagogical outlook on things, a "teacherly" way of viewing the world?[8]

When we recognize the great variety of teachers the world over,

---

[6]The question of whether and how to recapture the freshness of vision we once had as children is a topic of great interest to many, from the Romantic poets of the nineteenth century to many of today's psychotherapists.

[7]This point is made with considerable force in Elliot W. Eisner's *The Educational Imagination* (New York: Macmillan Publishing Co., 1979). See in particular Chapter 9, "On the Art of Teaching."

[8]This question is treated in an intriguing manner in J.M. Stephens, *The Process of Schooling: a Psychological Examination* (New York: Holt, Rinehart and Winston, 1967). Stephens hypothesizes that people with certain proclivities and impulses, such as the proclivity to detect errors and the impulse to correct them, are naturally drawn to teaching.

it is hard to imagine that such a diverse group might be bound together by any single perspective on their work, an outlook that would characterize them all. At the same time, by staying at a rather low level of generalization and by focusing on perception alone, we can observe distinctions between the ways "experts" and "laymen" look at things that would seem to hold true for the difference between teachers and nonteachers as well.

For example, other things being equal, we might expect the expert's view to be more differentiated than that of the layman. We would expect him or her to have a "finer" than ordinary perception of the object of his expertise, to see it in greater detail. We would also expect such a person to have a "quicker" vision as well, to be able to take in a lot of information at a glance, homing in quickly on features worthy of special attention. We would expect the expert to have an eye for irregularities and trouble spots. We would also expect him to see opportunities missed by others. He or she would be expected to be more "future-oriented," to see possibilities where others see none.

We would also expect the expert to see things in perspective, to know, for example, whether to treat something with alarm or more routinely. In other words, we would not expect the expert to get "rattled" by the unexpected quite as easily as might the layman. In sum, we normally expect the expert to be more thoughtful than the nonexpert about things, not in the sense of thinking *more*, but rather in the sense of thinking *differently*. Moreover, this thoughtfulness can be reflected in a variety of ways.

As applied to teachers and teaching, this set of expectations yields an image of the seasoned teacher that distinguishes him or her, at least in principle, from laymen in general and possibly even from novice teachers. Expert teachers "see more" than do nonexperts. They are alive to the latent pedagogical possibilities in the events they witness. Within a classroom setting, they anticipate what is going to happen. They can spot an inattentive student a mile off. They can detect signs of incipient difficulty. Their senses are fully tuned to what is going on around them. They are not easily rattled. As younger students sometimes swear is true, they behave as though they had eyes in the back of their heads.

Is this image of expert teaching accurate? Are all seasoned teachers really like that? Are any of them? In short, are we talking about what is or what ought to be?

The quick sketch given here admittedly comes closer to the "ought" than the "is" of teachers and teaching. At the same time, it is not entirely a fiction. It reminds me sufficiently of teachers I have known that I will defend it as a model realizable in the here and now.

But even more important than whether many or most teachers come to resemble our hypothetical expert, how does such a perspective on teaching address the array of questions treated in this chapter? Of special interest is what it seems to say about the relationship between what a teacher *does* and what he or she *thinks*.

I now return for a final time to the rather lighthearted discussions that took place in the nursery school, and readily admit, though it should be abundantly obvious, that I knew all along a person could not become a nursery school teacher simply by learning how to hold a book while reading a story to children or by bending this way or that while talking or listening to a small child. The teachers knew that as well, of course, which explains their willingness to go along with the fun. They knew, and I knew, that to be a real nursery school teacher one had to see and to react in a certain spirit or manner to a special portion of the world—rooms full of three- and four-year-olds. Specific skills, such as knowing how to make playdough or how to bandage a cut knee, had an important place in that world, as we might expect them to, but to mistake such skills for the heart of the matter, as my lunchtime boast seemed to do, was—well, just laughable, that's all.

Is the situation drastically different with other types of teaching? My own experience in colleges and universities leads me to say no. There too the difference between the novice (who for rhetorical purposes has been likened to an imposter) and his or her more experienced colleagues turns out to be less a matter of skill than one of feeling and acting at home within a particular instructional milieu.

This sense of "being at home" in the classroom is hard to specify, I admit, but as a psychological state it is quite genuine all the same. One of the nursery school teachers nearly referred to it directly when she said, "Well, even if the imposter never gives himself away, *he* knows he doesn't belong there."

III.

The final question to be raised in this chapter is the one toward which my discussion with the nursery school teachers pointed but never reached: Is there some ultimate, non-modifiable definition of teaching (*true* teaching, let's call it) that we can discover through empirical and/or logical maneuvering?

We need first to acknowledge that the question is academic, in the sense that teachers themselves seem not to worry about it very much. Except when prodded by one of their instructors while in training or by a school administrator with nothing better to do, most teachers I have known seldom wonder aloud about the *true* meaning of teaching. Like other kinds of practitioners the world over, they usually are too busy doing what they have to do to worry about formal definitions of their practice.

Yet there are groups of people—educational philosophers among them—who do have time for such matters and who look upon it as part of their professional responsibility to answer the definitional question, whether practicing teachers are interested or not. Moreover, the answers they offer are more than academic exercises. These answers appear in textbooks and other "official" documents where they may potentially influence how teachers and others think about teaching.

This is hardly the place to examine all such efforts in detail. However, I would like to touch upon three different approaches to the task of determining once and for all what teaching is or should be. In my judgment, each of the three is seriously flawed, yet each builds from a foundational premise that in certain respects is quite appealing. Each strikes me as contributing to an understanding of why the search for a final, logically airtight definition of teaching is not only a futile undertaking but may even be harmful if allowed to legislate what teachers themselves must believe about their work.

I will call these three approaches to the definition of teaching the *generic*, the *epistemic*, and the *consensual*. The meaning of those terms will become clear in the exposition to follow.

What I call a *generic* approach to the definition of teaching works like this: It begins by insisting that there be an important difference between a definition of teaching, on the one hand, and the perform- ance of teaching on the other. This distinction is important, for it divides the labor of speaking authoritatively about teaching between two groups of professionals—educational philosophers and educa- tional researchers. From this point of view it is the job of the philosophers to propose a definition of teaching that is sufficiently general to cover whatever future research might discover about the right *way* to teach. The job of researchers, in turn, is to discover answers to questions about how teaching should proceed. The result of the former effort will be singular and universal; that of the latter, plural and particular. Here is the way one well-known educational philosopher, B.O. Smith, poses the problem and then goes on to solve it.

> "The way in which teaching is or can be performed," Smith tells us, is mistaken for teaching itself. In its generic sense, teaching is a system of actions intended to induce learning. So defined, teaching

is everywhere the same, irrespective of the cultural context in which it occurs. But these actions may be performed differently from culture to culture or from one individual to another within the same culture, depending on the state of knowledge about teaching and the teacher's pedagogical knowledge and skill. Didactics, or the science and art of teaching, are not the same as the actions which they treat. A definition of teaching as such, which packs a set of biases about how these actions are to be conducted, confuses teaching with its science and its art."[9]

This approach has a degree of common sense about it that must be acknowledged at the start. Teaching may be variably performed, that much is certainly true. Thus it makes good sense to seek a definition of teaching that is flexible but not so broad that it embraces everything under the rubric of "teaching." The question is whether Smith's definition of teaching as a system of actions intended to induce learning fits the bill. I fear it does not.

Consider, for instance, the giving of medicine to a hyperactive child in order to calm him or her down so that she or he might benefit from instruction. This certainly must be acknowledged as a system of actions intended to induce learning, must it not? But is it an instance of teaching? I suspect few would be willing to consider it so.

And what of the work of school administrators? Much of what they do would certainly conform to Smith's generic definition of teaching. But, again, who would want to call most principals or superintendents teachers? I for one would not, and once again, I suspect most people would agree.

So Smith's generic definition of teaching, if I understand it correctly, is far too broad to be of much use. All of teaching fits within it, sure enough, but so do many other activities that we do not want to confuse with teaching.

And even if the definition could be tightened to exclude those activities we do not want,[10] it is still hard to imagine that such a definition might be useful in practice. Suppose we could define teaching generically—that is, say nothing about how teaching should be done but differentiate between teaching and all other activities. What would we do with such a definition once we had it? What

---

[9]B. Othanel Smith, "A concept of teaching," in B. Othanel Smith and Robert H. Ennis (eds.), *Language and Concepts in Education* (Chicago: Rand McNally, 1961), 87–88.

[10]One way to do so would be to restrict the meaning of the verb "induce" to that of "moving by persuasion or influence." But even this narrowing of normal usage seems to leave the definitional door too far ajar.

questions of consequence would it help to answer? That I can think of none may reflect nothing more than my lack of imagination, but it is enough to leave me dubious about the promise of a *generic* approach to the definition of teaching.

An *epistemic*, as contrasted with a *generic*, definition of teaching links the activity to the concept of knowledge propounded by most modern epistemologists. In this view, knowledge is understood to be "evidentially supported belief." If we add to that understanding the corollary that teaching is primarily concerned with the transmission of such knowledge, we can begin to see that it *logically entails* certain kinds of actions and not others.

For example, it obliges teachers to provide grounds or reasons for the beliefs they seek to inculcate in their students. It requires them to be respectful of the truth and to be prepared at all times to reevaluate their own beliefs in the light of new evidence and in the face of fresh argument. It also demands that they seek to develop in each student his or her own capacity to test the worthiness of everything taught.

These obligations have nothing to do with personal choice or preference. Like a geometer's proof, they flow naturally from the starting premises of the argument, which say that teaching has to do with the spread of knowledge as contemporaneously defined and with the conditions conducive to that end.

From those same premises there follows a list of "don'ts" as well as "dos." Teachers committed to viewing knowledge as "evidentially supported belief" are also obliged not to intimidate, or threaten, or lie, or propagandize. They are sworn to avoid at all costs anything known to be inimical to the conduct of human inquiry and to the motivational spirit which animates it. Should they violate either set of these obligations, the positive or the negative, they step beyond the parameters of teaching as circumscribed by an epistemic definition.

This approach to a definition of teaching is attractive in several ways. To begin with, it is more philosophically sophisticated than is the generic approach. It does not so readily embrace features that teaching shares with many other activities. Instead, it tries to identify what is unique to teaching, what distinguishes it from all or almost all other activities. Also, it speaks out on behalf of a conception of teaching that has many supporters, both within the profession and outside of it. The teacher as a purveyor of knowledge, in the sense explicated, is an ancient and honored image of what teachers and teaching are all about.

At the same time, the epistemic view is not without difficulties of its own. For one thing, it does not address educational goals that are only indirectly associated with the transmission of knowledge. It may well be that the development of attitudes, interests, values, and the like can be reduced to knowledge of one sort or another, but I doubt that many teachers regard those goals in that way.

Finally, the epistemic approach to a definition of teaching leaves us in an awkward position with respect to teachers, past and present, who did and do indeed indoctrinate, intimidate, propagandize, and goodness knows what else, thinking it quite proper to do so.[11] What shall we say of them? Here is an answer given by Thomas Green, another educational philosopher, who is at the same time a strong advocate of an epistemic approach to the definition of teaching.

> Lying, propagandizing, slander and threat of physical violence are not teaching activities, although they may be ways of influencing persons' beliefs or shaping their behavior. We know *in fact* that these activities are excluded from the concept of teaching with as much certainty as we know that training and instruction are included. [Emphasis added][12]
>
> It is a matter of no consequence that there have been societies which have extended the concept of teaching . . . [to include such practices] . . . That propaganda, lies, threats, and intimidation have been used as methods of education is not doubted. But the conclusion warranted by this fact is not that teaching includes such practices, but that education may. Propaganda, lies, threats are more or less effective means of influencing and shaping beliefs and patterns of behavior. It follows that teaching is not the only method of education. It does not follow that the use of propaganda, lies and threats are methods of teaching.[13]

We can treat undesirable actions on the part of teachers as instances of nonteaching, but one wonders what we gain by such a move. What it does, so far as I can tell, is sweep an interesting question under the rug, that question being: Why might teachers, past and present, have put such tactics to use in the first place? To imply that they did so out of ignorance, that they lacked knowledge of the true meaning of teaching, seems a bit condescending, to say

---

[11]For a powerful statement on behalf of teachers as indoctrinators and propagandizers, see George C. Counts, *Dare the Schools Build a New Social Order?* (New York: John Day Co., 1932).

[12]Thomas F. Green, "A typology of the teaching concept." In Macmillan and Nelson, *Concepts of Teaching*, 36–37. (Italics added.)

[13]Ibid., 37.

the least. It also begs the question of how or whether we can have a "true" definition of the term.

The third approach (I call it *consensual*) to the question of how to define teaching is close in spirit to the second, but more accommodating in tone and less rigidly tied to epistemological claims. It allows for many ways of teaching, but it seeks to distinguish between those that are *standard* and those that are *nonstandard*. Israel Scheffler, yet another educational philosopher, is an articulate spokesman for this point of view. "Teaching may, to be sure, proceed by various methods," Scheffler begins,

> but some ways of getting people to do things are excluded from the *standard range* of the term 'teaching.' To teach, *in the standard sense*, is at some points at least to subject oneself to the understanding and independent judgment of the pupil, to his demand for reasons, to his sense of what constitutes an adequate explanation. To teach someone that such and such is the case is not merely to try to get him to believe it: deception for example, is not a method or mode of teaching . . . To teach is thus, *in the standard use of the term*, to acknowledge the 'reason' of the pupil, i.e. his demand for and judgment of reasons, even though such demands are not uniformly appropriate at every phase of the teaching interval. [Emphasis added][14]

In what kind of society would Scheffler's version of teaching flourish? "It would be a place," he tells us,

> where the culture itself institutionalizes reasoned procedures in its basic spheres, where it welcomes the exercise of criticism and judgment, where, that is to say, it is a democratic culture in the strongest sense. To support the widest diffusion of teaching as a model of cultural renewal is, in effect, to support something peculiarly consonant with the democratization of culture and something that poses a threat to cultures whose basic social norms are institutionally protected from criticism.[15]

So in the final analysis it is only in a democratic society, or one in the process of becoming so, that teaching in Scheffler's sense of the term can be carried on. His standard use of the term is consensual in the dictionary sense of "existing or made by mutual consent without

---

[14] Israel Scheffler, *The Language of Teaching* (Springfield, Ill.: Charles C. Thomas, 1960), 57–58. (Italics added.)

[15] Ibid, 59.

the intervention of any act of writing." But the consenting parties, in Scheffler's view, must be like-minded in broad political terms.

The notion that teaching in its "truest" sense can be carried on only in a democratic society may be comforting to those of us who believe we live in such a society. But how fair is it to restrict by definition the idea of teaching to a particular political context? Is there not something a trifle chauvinistic about such a move?

Of course we should feel free to criticize the way teaching is carried out in societies other than our own, just as we should here at home. But I fail to see how it helps to approach this job of criticism armed with a definition that to start with rules out the possibility of our calling what goes on in non-democratic countries "teaching." Scheffler dodges this question, at least in part, by his willingness to speak of *non-standard* teaching. Yet, reading his words carefully, I must conclude that what he means by the *non-standard* form of the activity is almost not teaching at all.[16]

There is much to be said for both the epistemic and the consensual approaches to the definition of teaching, as this brief exposition sought to make clear. Each rests on a premise that many of today's teachers are almost certain to find attractive. It makes good sense to think that teaching is centrally concerned with the transmission of knowledge, as the epistemic approach insists we do. It is also appealing to think that teaching is a kind of emancipatory activity, either sustaining a democratic society or paving the way for its emergence, as the consensual approach requires.

But in the final analysis both views turn out to be more limiting than edifying. We must ask, why should teaching be perceived solely in terms of its contribution to the transmission of knowledge? And why must it be confined to the kind of teaching that typifies democratic societies (if any kind actually does)? But if we reject such limitations are we not forced back to a generic definition of the kind Smith proposed, one so general as to be useless? Not necessarily.

There is, I would suggest, a fourth approach to the question of how teaching is defined, an approach that I call *evolutionary*. The term comes from Stephen Toulmin, who describes such a view in the following way.

---

[16]There is a real question whether it is possible to define teaching ontologically—in a way that speaks of its true meaning or essence—without also getting entangled with a definition that is axiological—one that involves the meaning of "good" teaching. For a discussion of this issue see W. A. Hart, "Is teaching what the philosophers understand by it?" *British Journal of Educational Studies* 24, number 2 (June 1976): 155–170.

A properly evolutionary way of dealing with experience obliges us to recognize that no event or process has any single unambiguous description: we describe any event in different terms, and view it as an element in a different network of relations, depending on the standpoint from which—and the purposes for which—we are considering it. [17]

What would be the consequences of looking upon teaching in this way? We begin by conceding that there is no unequivocal definition of teaching that holds for all time and all places. What we accept as a satisfactory view of the process today within our society may not be the definition agreed upon in another time or another culture. But that does not mean that everyone holding different views, whether in the past or the present, can now be called wrong. What such an evolutionary view commits us to is neither the truth nor the falsity of any single definition; rather, it is an attempt to locate teaching within what Toulmin calls "a network of relations." Its place within that network is its ultimate source of meaning and significance.

Lest this sound far too abstract to be of practical help, let us move closer to the everyday world of teaching to see what the possible consequences of such a view might be. First of all, it would put to rest all ontological questions of the kind I discussed with teachers during my early days as a nursery school principal—questions of who is real and who is fake, whether one is really teaching as opposed to doing something else that might resemble teaching but is not the genuine article, and so forth.

This does not mean that people could no longer lie about their teaching abilities or falsify their credentials to make people believe they have had training when they have not. In short, it does not eliminate the possibility of frauds and fakes within the ranks of teachers. It does help us see that what is fraudulent in such situations is not teaching *per se* but the claim to competence.

To put the argument in a nutshell, there is no such thing as "genuine" teaching. There is only an activity that people call teaching, which can be viewed from a variety of critical perspectives. Sometimes the criticism that teaching can undergo leads us to conclude that the person performing the activity, or claiming to be able to perform it, has deceived us in some way. Such deceptions are rare, we would hope, but they have been known to happen.

---

[17] Stephen Toulmin, "The charm of the scout," *New York Review of Books*, April 3, 1980, 38.

Of far more practical importance than anything involving "genuine" teaching are questions of "good" and "poor" teaching. What does an "evolutionary" view of the process enable us to say about that? It leads to the understanding that we can make few if any judgments about the quality of teaching without reference to the context in which the action takes place; "context" is understood to cover far more than the physical setting of the action. The phrase "cultural context" comes closer to the meaning being sought here. It includes the awarenesses, presuppositions, expectations, and everything else that impinges upon the action or that contributes to its interpretation by the actors themselves and by outsiders as well.

Consider this example. Teachers of approximately a hundred years ago routinely applied hickory sticks to the backsides of recalcitrant or misbehaving students, or so we are told. What shall we, today, make of that fact? Shall we think of our colleagues of years ago as having been poor teachers for behaving as they did?

I find that too hasty and harsh a judgment. Moreover, I see nothing to be gained by it. To learn something from the past it seems to me far more fruitful to ask why that particular practice (and others like it) have gradually died out. Such a question is also much more in keeping with what I am calling an "evolutionary" point of view. An understanding of the demise of the hickory stick yields a correlative understanding of why many related practices have disappeared as well.

But what about contemporary practice? Does an evolutionary and contextual outlook leave us powerless to criticize what goes on today? Does it get stalled at the level of "mere understanding," leaving the tough job of being critical and of taking a stand on issues to someone else?

Not at all. There is no incompatibility between understanding an activity and either approving or disapproving it. Here an example might help. Suppose we learn of a teacher who seeks to win a student over to his or her own point of view through deception of one kind or another. Does not such a practice surpass understanding and call for immediate censure? Scheffler, for one, would say so, for he explicitly tells us that "deception . . . is not a method or mode of teaching." But what if we learn that the teacher in question is none other than Jean Jacques Rousseau and the student his famous fictional creation, Emile?[18]

---

[18] *Emile* is full of instances in which the teacher seeks to deceive his pupil in some way, to achieve what he alleges to be a pedagogical end.

In such an instance would we not be better advised to try to understand what Rousseau was up to and why he did what he did *before* we conclude that censure is in order? What applies to fiction holds in real life as well. Confronted with any instance of teaching we might either praise or blame, we must always ask: What are the circumstances of the case? Why were these actions undertaken?[19]

Our answers to such questions no more prevent us from censuring any particular teacher (or a whole nation full of them, if need be) than does an investigation of an alleged crime prevent us from punishing the criminal. Indeed, the process of deliberating on such matters resembles that of case law more closely than it does that of establishing the proof of a theorem in geometry or mathematics. What grows out of such a procedure is not a definition that will stand forever. Rather, it is an argument and its defense.[20]

Who are real teachers and what is real teaching? There are no such things, says the person who has adopted an evolutionary point of view. There are interpretations of events, including those in which teachers are the central actors. There are arguments that can be made on behalf of this or that teaching practice. Some arguments are better than others. Doubtless there are some practices that most of us teaching today would defend. Part of our professional responsibility is to get on with that defense. If we are lucky, as I was during my fledgling days as a nursery school principal, the task of deciding who is and who is not a teacher, though serious enough in the long run, will have its lighter moments as well.

---

[19] For an interesting discussion of how the case study point of view has moved from medicine to ethical theory and has rejuvenated the latter, see Stephen Toulmin, "How medicine saved the life of ethics," *Perspectives in Biology and Medicine* 25, number 4 (Summer 1982): 736–750.

[20] For an insightful treatment of the distinction between logical reasoning and the kind of reasoning employed in everyday argumentation, see Stephen Toulmin, *The Uses of Argument* (Cambridge: Cambridge University Press, 1958).

5 THE FUTURE OF TEACHING

THE SUBSTANCE OF THIS CHAPTER revolves around two questions. One inquires about the past; the other about the future. The first asks whether teaching, the world over, is conducted with any greater skill and sensitivity than was true generations ago. In short, does the practice of teaching show signs of historical progress? The second asks whether there is still room for improvement. "Can teaching be done any better than we do it today? If so, how?" would be the most direct way of putting it. My answer to both questions is affirmative but qualified. I shall argue that teaching *has* improved over the centuries. It is likely to continue to do so as far into the future as we might care to gaze. Our optimism must be tempered, however, by the realization that educational progress is by no means inevitable, nor is its future direction completely clear.

I.

Those who seek to convince others that the quality of teaching has either improved or deteriorated over time commonly do so by making some kind of side-by-side comparison of today's teaching practices with those of a bygone era, such as that of our parents or grandparents. Moreover, instead of simply calling these practices the older and the newer ways of teaching, they often tag them with more evaluative labels like "old-fashioned" and "modern" or "traditional" and "progressive." More often than not, such descriptions are as much caricatures as they are realistic depictions of how teaching is actually carried on. The best of them, however, like all good caricatures, contain their share of the truth all the same.

In his book *Experience and Education*, which appeared in 1938, John Dewey provides a good example of how such a comparison typically works. What he has to say about the subject has been said by many others before and since, but seldom as succinctly.

Dewey begins by observing that "[m]ankind likes to think in

terms of extreme opposites." Educational philosophy, he points out, is no exception to that rule. Indeed, the history of educational theory, as Dewey views it,

> is marked by opposition between the idea that education is devel-
> opment from within and that it is formation from without; that it is
> based upon natural endowments and that education is a process of
> overcoming natural inclination and substituting in its place habits
> acquired under external pressure.[1]

He then goes on to remark that at the time in which he wrote this recurring opposition had taken the form of a contrast between traditional and progressive education. He proceeds to spell out that contrast in some detail.

Dewey depicts the basic tenets of traditional education as follows:

> The subject matter of education consists of bodies of information and
> of skills that have been worked out in the past; therefore, the chief
> business of the school is to transmit them to the new generation. In
> the past, there have also been developed standards and rules of
> conduct; moral training consists in forming habits of action in con-
> formity with these rules and standards. Finally, the general pattern
> of school organization (by which I mean the relations of pupils to one
> another and to the teachers) constitutes the school a kind of insti-
> tution sharply marked off from other social institutions.[2]

These three characteristics, Dewey goes on,

> fix the aims and methods of instruction and discipline. The main
> purpose or objective is to prepare the young for future responsibil-
> ities and for success in life, by means of acquisition of the organized
> bodies of information and prepared forms of skill which comprehend
> the material of instruction. Since the subject-matter as well as
> standards of proper conduct are handed down from the past, the
> attitude of pupils must, upon the whole, be one of docility, recep-
> tivity, and obedience. Books, especially textbooks, are the chief
> representatives of the lore and wisdom of the past, while teachers are
> the organs through which pupils are brought into effective connec-
> tion with the material. Teachers are the agents through which
> knowledge and skills are communicated and rules of conduct en-
> forced.[3]

---

[1] John Dewey, *Experience and Education* (New York: Collier Books, 1938), 17.
[2] Ibid., 17–18.
[3] Ibid., 18.

Dewey next explains that the rise of what was then called the "new" education and "progressive" schools had been in response to a discontent with the traditional view. He then proceeds to formulate the philosophy of education implicit in the practices of the "new" education. These were the principles that Dewey believed were common to the operation of the several different kinds of "progressive" schools then in existence.

> To imposition from above, [he began,] is opposed expression and cultivation of individuality; to external discipline is opposed free activity; to learning from texts and teachers, learning from experience; to acquisition of isolated skills and techniques by drill, is opposed acquisition of them as means of attaining ends which make direct vital appeal; to preparation for a more or less remote future is opposed making the most of opportunities of present life; to static aims and materials is opposed acquaintance with a changing world. [4]

Dewey's summary of the historical opposition within education —its polarization into the developoment-from-within, versus formation-from-without, points of view—is admirably concise. So too is his depiction of the status of that historical dichotomy in his own day. But, concise though it may be, I find his overview to be deficient in certain respects all the same. Let me quickly name my misgivings.

For one thing, I don't like the labels Dewey chooses to apply to the two educational outlooks. For another, I would highlight rather different aspects of the polarity Dewey sketches, making the opposing views somewhat less at swords' points. Finally, given the historical longevity of these contrary points of view, I would raise a question that Dewey seems not to have addressed in the book I've cited here: Why has the debate lasted so long? Each of these three changes that I would like to make in Dewey's perspective moves us a step closer to answering the two key questions with which I began.

First: to get rid of the labels Dewey used. I want to abandon the term "traditional" for what is allegedly the older of the two points of view because both outlooks have been around for such a very long time (as Dewey himself rightly points out) that each by now is something like a tradition in its own right. Thus as I see it, there exist at least two traditional outlooks on educational affairs, two distinguishably different vantage points from which to view the goals, the conduct, and the outcomes of teaching. To call but one of them "traditional" is to imply that the other one, whatever we may call it, does not also have deep historical roots, which, in fact, it clearly does.

---

[4] Ibid., 19–20.

I do not wish to call the second and allegedly more recent point of view "progressive," simply because the application of such a label amounts to prejudging what seems to me to be a key question— whether the educational outlook of those who call themselves progressive truly deserves such an accolade. Do the so-called "progressive" methods of teaching constitute genuine progress? To leave room for a consideration of that question, I prefer to eschew all terms that implicitly or explicitly answer it in advance.

But if not "traditional" and "progressive," then what shall we name these divergent points of view? Quite frankly, I don't think it matters terribly what we call them so long as we don't think of one as traditional and the other not, and so long as we keep an open mind (at least for a time) about the relative merits of each. For reasons soon to become apparent, I prefer to call them the "conservative" and the "liberal" outlooks on educational affairs; if the political overtones of those two terms are too objectionable, as they may be to some, I would accept a more neutral pair of terms, such as "old" and "new," just so long as we remember that what is being called "new" under such an arrangement is really not so new after all.

More important than what we call the two perspectives outlined by Dewey is how we see them relating to each other. Dewey, we recall, portrayed them as *opposing* points of view, almost exact opposites. He depicted one as stressing docility; the other, activity; one as oriented toward the past, the other, toward the future; and so on. Dewey did not firmly situate himself on either side of this dichotomy, I must point out, though it seems to me quite evident that his sympathies lie with the "new" education, as opposed to the "old."[5]

Such bipolar depictions may highlight genuine differences in educational outlook among protagonists in the real world, but I have trouble with them all the same. Like Dewey himself, I find them too stark to capture the subtlety of the many arguments taking place within the educational community at home and abroad. Moreover, I fear that such quick sketches, even when deftly done, too often have the undesirable effect of solidifying and even deepening whatever cleavages of opinion already exist about such matters.

To prevent that happening or at least to lessen its likelihood, I would like to present a picture of the discord within the educational

---

[5]Indeed, throughout his life as a philosopher Dewey strove to eliminate such dichotomous ways of thinking—a goal that comes close to expressing the heart of his philosophy. But these black and white conceptions, Dewey reminded us all, were the way mankind has thought and continues to think about such matters.

community that is somewhat less black-and-white than Dewey's. Mine contains several shades of gray. I would begin my sketch by calling attention to two lines of advance within teaching, moving toward a pair of goals that nearly everyone seems to accept, at least in principle, no matter what other differences of opinion might separate them. True, disagreement about these matters has been rife over the years and remains so today. But much of that disagreement, as we shall see, centers on questions of feasibility and timing—technical matters for the most part—rather than on the goals *per se*.

The more peripheral of these two goals, as it stands within the tradition of educational thought, is the reduction, if not the elimination, of all unnecessary discomfort associated with the process of learning. I shall call this effort "the search for painless pedagogy." That phrase may sound too journalistic to be taken seriously by some readers, but soon I hope to rid it of that taint by showing how deep its roots are in the history of educational reform.

The more central of the two goals toward which teaching seems to have been headed over the years with the tacit, if not explicit, consent of almost all concerned, is the gradual freeing of each student from his or her dependence on pedagogical authority altogether. The goal, in short, is personal independence in attaining knowledge and skills, forming opinions, tastes, and so forth. Efforts in this direction constitute a move toward self-governance for all learners. That "self-governance" movement, as I shall call it, comprises a major theme within the larger story of how teaching has changed over the centuries. Together with the search for painless pedagogy it provides a pair of common goals toward which many who are otherwise divided can mutually strive.

II.

As I have already said, the search for painless pedagogy has inspired educational reformers throughout modern history. For example, it is at the heart of the teachings of Comenius, who in 1657 proposed a system of teaching that, as he put it, "shall be conducted without blows, rigor or compulsion, as gently and pleasantly as possible."[6] That identical vision or something very close to it weaves its way down through the centuries to our own time. Comenius was not by any means the first to voice such an aspiration. Confucius

---

[6]M.W. Keatinge (trans.), *The Great Didactic of John Amos Comenius* (New York: Russell and Russell, 1910), 81.

called for making learning "gentle" and "easy" as far back as the fifth century B.C. and so have countless other educational reformers since then. Some have pressed beyond that goal to insist that learning be not only easy but actually enjoyable, even *fun*!

How might such a goal be accomplished? There are two quite different ways of going about it, each with innumerable variations. One approach calls for injecting more pleasure into the learning process than was there to begin with. A pejorative term for some forms of that practice is "sugarcoating." The introduction of game-like activities into the process of instruction (an idea suggested by John Locke, among others) provides a good example of this first approach. (Locke, writing in the late seventeenth century, thought that reading might be taught by pasting letters on the sides of four or five dice, which the student would toss and then try to figure out how many words could be spelled using only the letters that came out on top—sort of an early version of one of today's many word games that parents sometimes buy in the hope of making their children proficient readers.) The other approach is to rid the process of teaching and learning of discomfort already there. Calling for an end to corporal punishment in the classroom, as Comenius did, is an obvious example of this second strategy.

Of course, there are more subtle ways of making learning pleasurable than by introducing games into the classroom, just as there are more refined ways of eliminating pain, beyond prohibiting the use of corporal punishment. Illustrated textbooks, friendliness from teachers and administrators, comfortable chairs and desks, even pictures on the wall and a fresh coat of paint on the ceiling, might all contribute to an overall feeling of pleasure on the part of students and teachers alike. A full listing of all such attempt to improve the sheer physical comfort of being in school would fill volumes.

Beyond these more or less direct actions aimed at making life in school or college more pleasant, there are many indirect ways to the same end. For example, if there were no way to eliminate the pain associated with a certain kind of learning, the next best thing would be to shorten the period of suffering. One alternative might be to increase the rate of teaching, the way a dentist might use a fast drill to get the worst over as quickly as possible. (Various forms of so-called "cram" courses, such as those used for intensive study of a foreign language, are the educational equivalent of the dentist's fast drill.) We might also make the experiences of discomfort briefer and scatter them over a longer period of time than they might otherwise take, administering the medicine in small doses, so to speak.

Should these and other attempts to reduce excessive discomfort all fail or seem inadvisable for one reason or another, we can always abandon the learning objective entirely or make it optional, as in schools that either do away with the so-called "hard" subjects, such as math and foreign languages, or make them elective. Because difficulty is so often the cause of discomfort in learning situations, one sure-fire way to get rid of the latter is by getting rid of the former. (This is seldom the soundest option from an educational standpoint, of course, but it certainly has been known to happen, as we will be forced to acknowledge when we consider the continuing controversy between proponents of the conservative and the liberal traditions within educational thought.)

Shifting now to the second of the two goals under discussion, that of increased self-governance on the part of the learner, here too we find a distinction between two different approaches to the problem. This time, however, the difference is not as simple as between adding on pleasure on the one hand, and subtracting discomfort on the other. Instead, we find that the goal of self-governance is made up of two distinct sub-goals, each of which can be considered on its own, even though their attainment may be jointly realized.

One of these sub-goals I shall call "learning to learn"; the other, "choosing to learn." The former concerns tools and resources instrumental to the realization of any and all learning goals. The latter concerns the specifics of putting those tools and resources to use.

The phrase "learning to learn" stands for what is done to equip the learner with the instrumentality of self-instruction. When successful, that process yields two different outcomes—one largely intellectual, the other much more broadly related to a person's total character. In intellectual terms the goal is to teach a person to reason, to make judgments, to develop sustained arguments, to criticize the arguments of others, and so forth. It also requires familiarizing the student with the use of all kinds of instructional materials—books, libraries, computers, and more—on which so much of today's learning depends. In short, it means teaching him or her to think and act independently in order to become more knowledgeable and to do so with ever-increasing power and skill.

In terms more dispositional than intellectual, it means equipping the would-be learner with those attitudinal and emotional attributes (including a few old-fashioned virtues, surprisingly enough) that predispose a person to use reason. These would include a keen sense of curiosity, a high degree of intellectual honesty, confidence in one's ability to acquire knowledge, a healthy degree of skepticism when confronted with the knowledge claims of others, and so forth. It also includes bolstering a student's strength and willingness to persevere in learning. Taken together, the cognitive and the dispositional components of learning to learn yield a person whose intellectual posture resembles that of independent learners the world over. Such a person consistently displays a readiness, even an eagerness, to grapple with intellectual challenges both large and small.

The phrase "choosing to learn," which covers the other portion of the learner's move toward self-governance, involves selecting the goals of learning, that is, choosing *what* is to be learned, whether with the help of teachers or on one's own. It means being free to decide what knowledge is worth possessing. On the negative side it also means choosing what *not* to learn, deciding when to *stop* learning, or when not to begin in the first place. It means having one's needs and interests, both short-term and long-term, serve as guides at crucial points in the learning process. The fully self-governing learner, in this view, is the person who is learning what he or she *wants* to learn while voluntarily submitting to whatever constraints that choice entails.

III.

I have just offered a brief sketch of the two historical trends within teaching that seem to me clearly discernible when viewed from a proper historical distance: a search for painless pedagogy and a move toward the learner's self-governance. Both these tendencies seem so clearly the right way to move that it becomes hard to imagine anyone opposing them. Who would call for more discomfort on the part of the learner than need be? Who would want the learner to remain servile to his or her teacher longer than is necessary? The answer is: no one, or at least no reasonable person. Painless, or near-painless pedagogy and the furtherance of learner's self-governance seem almost indisputable goals.

Yet we know that people do occasionally disagree about such matters. How is that possible? The principal explanation, it seems to me, is that people seldom disagree about the goals *per se*. Instead, what sets them apart are definitional questions on the one hand and technical considerations on the other.

Thus, I do not accept Dewey's image of an almost physical contest between rivals confronting each other from opposite corners of the ring. To be sure, there is rivalry among people who disagree on both painless pedagogy and learners' self-governance. I see it as a verbal squabble between a set of visionary, would-be reformers on the one hand and a bunch of Doubting Thomases on the other. The latter frequently complain not that the advocates of the "new" education are headed in the wrong direction but, rather, that they have become excessive in their zeal and have gone too far, too fast. Both the conservative and the liberal factions within the educational community seem to me committed to the elimination of *unnecessary* and *excessive* discomfort from the learning process and to freeing the learner from the domination of pedagogical authority as speedily as possible. Where they differ (sometimes quite radically) is in their definition of discomfort in the first place, of what pedagogical authority is absolutely necessary (if any at all), and so forth.

Let us turn temporarily from whatever controversy may exist among persons of good will as they address such questions in the abstract. We may reasonably ask where these reform efforts, along with those outlined by Dewey, have taken us. This is really a two-fold question. One side is purely descriptive, the other more normative. The former asks how far educational practice has moved in the directions indicated; the latter wants to know whether such movements can reasonably be classified as progress.

We can start with the descriptive question and concentrate on the part of it that asks whether pedagogy as practiced today is less discomforting than it once was. I see no answer other than yes, at least with respect to the changes that have taken place within American schools during the last hundred years, though I suspect the same may be true the world over. Consider first what has happened to teachers. At all levels of schooling they are kindlier, friendlier, less strict, less formal—in a word more humane—in their dealings with students than they once were or at least than their historical portraits show them to have been. The scowls and frowns of teachers past, if we can believe reports of what schools were like a few generations back, have gradually been replaced by the smiles and kindly looks of teachers present.

Without insisting on the literal truth of that transformation, nor claiming its effect to be uniform, even figuratively speaking, I would certainly say it is a reasonably accurate portrayal of what has actually come to pass. There *has* occurred a noticeable change in the "classroom climate," by which today's educators mean the emotional tone and tenor of the social environment within which instruction takes place. As gauged solely by the personal warmth and friendliness emanating from the teacher (as good a barometer as any, I would say), that climate over the years has become decidedly more hospitable and inviting than it once was.

Moreover, it is not just the teacher's disposition that has changed. More than frowns and sour looks have diminished in frequency. Gone, or fast disappearing, are hickory sticks, canes, slippers, paddles, and other items that once served as implements of corporal punishment. Gone too are dunce's caps, the punitive, repetitious writing of sentences on the blackboard, the penalty of standing in the corner for some trivial wrongdoing, and many other forms of public humiliation teachers used routinely in the not-too-distant past. In short, today's teachers behave better toward their students in any number of ways than did their counterparts in ages past.

We need not stop with teachers and their practices as we tally the ways in which the discomfort and displeasure associated with learning have gradually been reduced over the years. The entire school environment, from textbooks to classroom furniture, has undergone a similar transformation. The textbooks are more colorful, the furniture more comfortable. Even the heating and the lighting have improved. Look wherever we may, from floor to ceiling or anywhere in between, the conclusion is the same: Today's schools are just plain nicer places to be than they were in days gone by.

A parallel trend can be discerned in the movement toward the learner's self-governance. It applies to both "learning to learn" and "choosing to learn." Today's students at all levels of education are encouraged to be more independent as thinkers than were students of generations past. They are required to memorize less and to understand more. They are routinely encouraged to ask questions, to seek rational explanations, and thereby to challenge authority. They are increasingly permitted to make up their own minds with respect to what is true or false, a strong argument or a weak one. In short today's youngsters are taught to be more critical of everything they are told than was so in the past.[7] On "choosing to learn," the picture is even clearer. Students are offered more choices today than ever. Not only are they free to choose more, but they have more to choose from. Indeed, they are faced with a veritable cornucopia of educational choices almost from the start. Beginning with the "free play" activities of nursery school and kindergarten and culminating in the "electives" of high school and beyond, the choice of what to do and

---

[7]There is a serious question whether *all* of today's students are being treated in the manner described. There is evidence that many students from impoverished environments are not encouraged to be nearly as critical of authority and as independent in their thought as are those from more privileged circumstances. See, for example, Jeannie Oakes, *Keeping Track: How Schools Structure Inequality* (New Haven: Yale University Press, 1985). Nonetheless, I believe that greater numbers of students, irrespective of background, are being so treated than in generations past.

what to study in school (or what not to do and what not to study) is more in the hands of students today than it was ever in the past. Though that freedom remains curtailed by the fact of compulsory education and required courses of study, not to mention external pressures to study one subject rather than another, its gradual increase from generation to generation remains undeniable.[8]

What, then, does our brief and informal historical overview lead us to conclude? It reveals genuine movement in the direction of the two interrelated goals I have identified—one of making the entire process of schooling more pleasurable, the other of placing greater control of the process in the hands of students. Now we must ask whether such movement constitutes genuine progress. I announced at the start my own answer to that question, which was a qualified yes. Let me first explain my affirmative response and then go on to express my reservations.

In one sense it hardly seems necessary to defend the use of the term "progressive" in reference to the changes that I have described. They speak for themselves. If their worth is self-evident, so must be their status as genuine advances in our conduct of education. All we need to do is reiterate what they are: the gradual reduction of discomfort associated with learning and the expeditious liberation of the learner from unnecessary pedagogical constraints. Signs of progress? Of course they must be. Who could think otherwise? But the self-evident worth of these changes must itself not be allowed to escape scrutiny. We must ask what there is about such changes that makes us so sure of our judgment.

One contributing factor, I am convinced, is that these movements within our schools are not isolated phenomena. Instead, they are part of a much larger pattern of change within Western society in particular and possibly throughout the entire world. As institutions embedded within that larger social context, our schools and colleges, through their policies and practices, have to some extent mirrored what was going on within the broader society while at the same time contributing their own forward momentum to the force of events. Thus we judge them to be good, more or less automatically, because

---

[8] Insofar as teaching is concerned, this latter set of changes means that teachers no longer have the degree of authority they once had. No longer can they tell students precisely what to study every step of the way. Students now have more of a say in such matters than they once had. Most teachers today may not feel that gradual diminution of pedagogical authority as a loss; in fact, they may welcome it, but it does constitute an important change all the same.

we perceive them as being "in step with the times," moving in the same direction as are a vast number of other social practices and policies.

The exact character of that more massive historical flow is not easily captured in a few words. Many have tried, including John Dewey, who in his *School and Society* undertook "the effort to conceive what roughly may be termed the 'New Education' in the light of larger changes in society."[9] Chief among those changes, as Dewey saw them, was the Industrial Revolution, driven by the application of science to human affairs. This industrial revolution led in turn to what Dewey called "an intellectual revolution" that put learning "into circulation." "Knowledge is no longer an immobile solid," he declared, "it has been liquified. It is actively moving in all the currents of society itself."[10]

Though Dewey's formulation of these sweeping historical changes is helpful, I prefer a more recent one offered by the British critic, Raymond Williams. Williams terms his observations of change in Western society "the long revolution." Here is how he introduces the idea.

> It seems to me we are living through a long revolution which our best descriptions only in part interpret. It is a genuine revolution, transforming men and institutions; continually extended and deepened by the actions of millions, continually and variously opposed by explicit reaction and by the pressure of habitual forms and ideas. Yet it is a difficult revolution to define, and its uneven action is taking place over so long a period that it is almost impossible not to get lost in its exceptionally complicated process.[11]

That revolution, Williams next explains, is really three-fold. It includes a democratic revolution, an industrial revolution, and a cultural revolution. The last, which embraces teaching and schooling, is, Williams tells us, the most difficult of the three to interpret. But despite that difficulty, he insists,

> we must certainly see the aspiration to extend the active process of learning, with the skills of literacy and other advanced communication, to all people rather than to limited groups, as comparable in importance to the growth of democracy and the rise of scientific

---

[9]John Dewey, *School and Society* (Chicago: University of Chicago, 1900), 8.
[10]Ibid., 25.
[11]Raymond Williams, *The Long Revolution* (New York: Harper and Row, 1961), x.

industry. This aspiration has been and is being resisted, sometimes
openly, sometimes subtly, but as an aim it has been formally
acknowledged, almost universally . . .[12]

Whether or not we accept Williams's term, "the long revolution,"
for the phenomena in question there seems to me little room to
question his overall premise. A sweeping set of changes has indeed
transformed the Western world along the lines he describes, and they
seem to be happening elsewhere as well. Those changes, we need
hardly be reminded, are difficult to define and uneven in their
occurrence. It is, as Williams says, almost impossible not to get lost in
tracing their details.

What is important to note about these changes, insofar as they
affect our schools, is that any single advance we might identify can
also be seen as a manifestation of some larger trend. Thus to understand fully the gradual elimination of harsh pedagogical practices
(like the hickory stick, for example), we must see that it reflects the
same change in social conscience that in the United States and Britain
led to the emergence of child labor laws. The development of the
elective system in our high schools is a partial outgrowth of shifts in
public sentiment that make it seem right for today's middle-class
parents to give their teenagers the keys to the car. And so it goes with
almost every important educational change we might name, particularly those hailed as signs of progress. Examined with care, each
turns out to be a partial manifestation of some larger change within
the body politic.

This "embeddedness" of the changes I have described, that is,
their fit within a larger social and historical context, is part of what
makes us so quick to view them as progressive. The fact that they are
in tune with many other contemporaneous currents helps to confirm
that judgment. If that's the way the entire society is moving, we seem
to say to ourselves, there must be something right about it.

Yet it is also clear that such reasoning has its limits. If it did not
we would have to conclude that every social trend is in the right
direction in some sense, and we know that is false. Such knowledge
should give us pause in making any of our social judgments. It leads
me to list some of my own misgivings about the progressive nature of
the changes I have described.

One of the chief sources of those misgivings is remarked upon in

---

[12] Ibid., xi.

the two quotations by Raymond Williams. It is that the changes I have mentioned are "uneven," as he describes the broader ones. Another is that they are resisted, "sometimes openly, sometimes subtly," as Williams points out, a fact that may partially account for their unevenness. These twin facts about the so-called "cultural revolution" taking place within our midst ought to give us pause in two ways. First, though we may point properly with pride to signs of progress along the lines indicated when schools and colleges are viewed from an historical perspective, we must also acknowledge the harsh fact that there are many schools and classrooms today (some critics might say "most" rather than "many") whose climate is exceedingly discomforting to all within, students and teachers alike. There are also many educational settings today (again some might want to say "most") in which the conditions for cultivating intellectual independence and nurturing self-governing learners are almost totally absent. So though we may have come a long way from the days of hickory sticks and dunce's caps, I fear we still have a long way to go. That fact is sobering to say the least.

But there is another reason why I hesitate to fire off salutes in celebration of the progress we have made so far. I can easily envision certain conditions under which my support of the changes that have been discussed would turn to opposition. The conservative viewpoint, I find, becomes quite appealing if presented in the right light. Acknowledging that, I am forced to part company with Dewey on this point. For he presented the "traditional" position so unsympathetically that I can't imagine any educator, save an out-and-out cartoon character like Dickens's Mr. Gradgrind, who would assume it willingly.

Such extremes are easily lampooned, as Dickens and others have done deftly. But they are easily dismissed as well. No one except a sadist would advocate the introduction of discomfort and suffering into the educational process for their own sake. Nor would anyone in his or her right mind recommend keeping students dutifully servile to their teachers a day longer than is necessary. But the crucial question, which quickly emerges when all cartoons are laid aside, is how much discomfort *can* be eliminated from the educative process without risking the loss of something even more important than relative comfort: education itself? Similarly, we might wonder if students could possibly be pressed to be more self-governing than is good for them, given the limits of their budding ability to weigh the long-term consequences of their actions. We can phrase such questions in terms of the ethical limits of teaching as a human endeavor—its professional boundaries, so to speak. How, if at all, can those boundaries be violated?

Here a comparison with a more homely enterprise may help. Think of the lifelong effort to achieve painless dentistry. That goal has not yet been reached, as most of us can readily testify, yet we also must admit that the dental profession is certainly much closer to it than it was a generation or two ago. But for all the progress toward making dentistry painless, we have little question that there are limits to that search. To take the extreme case, no one but a fool would suggest that painless dentistry be achieved by abandoning the profession entirely! More realistically, what responsible dentist would think of putting the reduction of discomfort ahead of the primary goal of caring for his or her patient's teeth? To be true to their calling, dentists and all other professionals must maintain priorities. They are obliged above all to be true to their calling.

Teachers are in a similar position with respect to their practice. They too may wish to reduce the discomfort associated with their work, and they may also wish to free their students from the necessity of their services as soon as possible, just as dentists might do. But like all other professionals within the so-called healing arts they have an obligation to the principal goal of their practice, an obligation that must take precedence over such a secondary consideration as comfort and even over the rights of students to determine the course of their own education every step of the way. In short, teachers too have a calling to which they must be true. It is one of the profession's paramount responsibilities to be as articulate as possible about that calling, its means, and its ends.

Here we have the opening salvo of the conservative argument. The undesirability of student discomfort is not at issue, nor is the overall goal of developing independence in learners. The question is whether the reduction of discomfort can be and sometimes is purchased at the sacrifice of other goals more central to the teacher's task, and whether the same might occasionally be true of the self-governance of students.

Can learning become so easy and so much fun that it is no longer learning? Can students be given more freedom than they can reasonably handle? Those are the rhetorical questions the conscientious conservative asks. They are rhetorical because everyone knows that the answer to each has to be yes. If carried to an extreme the pursuit of pleasure as an accompaniment of learning *can* overshadow and even eclipse the pursuit of knowledge. In matters having to do with their education students *can* be given more freedom than they can handle judiciously. Thus the crucial question becomes not whether such limits exist—of course they do—but rather how to determine when they are being approached or exceeded.

Unfortunately, there is no surefire alarm system that will sound a warning whenever a teacher—or an entire school system, or a nation, for that matter—veers too far from the path of educational good sense and thereby risks abandoning the demands of teaching entirely. Though there may be some rules applicable across the board, the ultimate judgments have to be made case by case, I fear, and in many of those situations not everyone involved will always come to the same conclusion.

There are, however, some general considerations that have wide application for those making such judgments. Chief among these is the need to achieve and maintain a balanced perspective on all that it means to teach. That never-ending task is eased when we recognize some of the differences among teachers that have been highlighted in this chapter.

I have emphasized throughout that variations among teaching practices (whether we contrast those of today with some past era or simply review differences found at any one time) can be meaningfully grouped for purposes of analysis and discussion into two broad categories, one of which I have labelled "conservative," the other "liberal." That pair of categories roughly parallels those that Dewey called "traditional" and "progressive," but the match, as I have sought to make clear, is by no means exact. As I have already pointed out, one difference between Dewey's view and my own is that the distinction is not quite so black and white for me as it appears to have been for him. Yet even in my portrayal of the two outlooks there remain real differences between them all the same.

The emphasis on the conservative side is on the material to be learned. The focus is upon a funded body of knowledge and skills whose transmission to successive generations is essential to the maintenance of the social polity. The primary task of the teacher from this perspective is to ensure the safe passage of the known and the knowable from one generation to the next. On the liberal side the emphasis is on the learner as an individual. The focus is upon fostering a wide range of desirable human qualities of which knowledge *per se* is but one. The teacher's primary task from this perspective is to be a kind of midwife whose job is to assist in the birth of new personalities, new characters, new selves.

These brief descriptions may sound like nothing more than

reworked versions of the old distinction between subject-centered and child-centered teaching, and so they are in large measure. But the point I wish to make is rather different from that usually intended. Typically, the distinction is introduced to encourage teachers to abandon their subject-centered ways and become more child-centered in their outlook. What I want to suggest instead is that teachers need not make such a choice, that to the extent they do—becoming exclusively subject-centered or child-centered in their orientation— they risk stepping outside the boundaries of teaching entirely.

Earlier I called each of these two perspectives on teaching a tradition within the profession at large, each with its own history of accomplishments, its own spokesmen, its own canonical texts, and so forth. As a tradition, each comprises a subculture within the broader culture of teaching conceived of as a unified practice distinct from other forms of human endeavor. Now it is time to ask whether individual teachers must choose between these two traditions in deciding how they will go about their own work and where their own professional allegiances will lie. I think they need not, though I admit that the temptation to do so is often quite strong and for many teachers may well prove irresistible. Indeed, it well may be that each of us has some kind of a built-in proclivity toward one or the other of these perspectives on teaching, just as it has been said that all people lean toward being either Platonic or Aristotelian in their outlook on life. Perhaps we have no choice but to cleave to either the tough-minded or the tender-minded view of teaching, as William James might have called them.

But though we all may feel compelled to make such a choice, those of us who do so are well-advised to keep two considerations in mind. One is the recognition that both outlooks have legitimacy so long as neither is carried to an extreme. The other is the realization— all extremes aside—that the differences separating adherents of these two teaching traditions are far more matters of degree than of kind.

In sum, to be genuinely true to their calling, all teachers must be partially conservative and partially liberal in outlook. Though the historical drift of the profession, at least in recent years, may seem to have been in one direction only—toward a more liberal interpretation of teaching—the health and future development of teaching depend upon most teachers' maintaining a balanced view of both the means and the ends of pedagogy. Were he still among us, John Dewey would almost certainly agree.

6

THE MIMETIC
AND THE TRANSFORMATIVE:
ALTERNATIVE OUTLOOKS
ON TEACHING

THE GREEK SOPHIST PROTAGORAS allegedly claimed that on every subject two opposite statements could be made, each as defensible as the other. Whether or not he was right in a universal sense is something for logicians and rhetoricians to decide. However, insofar as the affairs of everyday life are concerned, he seems to have hit upon a fundamental truth, for we encounter daily all manner of "opposite statements," each with its share of supporters and critics.

As might be expected, education as a field of study is no exception to the rule. There too, differing outlooks, poles apart at first glance, are as common as elsewhere. Who, for example, is unfamiliar with the many verbal exchanges that have taken place over the years between "traditional" educators on the one side and their "progressive" opponents on the other, debates in which the merits of "child-centered" practices are pitted against those considered more "subject-centered"?

This final chapter introduces a dichotomy that encompasses the differences just named as well as others less familiar, though it is not usually talked about in the terms I will employ here. Indeed, the names of the two outlooks to be discussed have been purposely chosen so as to be *un*familiar to most followers of today's educational discussions and debates. My reason for this is not to introduce novelty for its own sake, much less to add glitter by using a pair of fancy terms. Instead, it is to avoid becoming prematurely embroiled in the well-known controversies associated with phrases like "child-centered" and "subject-centered," controversies that too often degenerate into mud-slinging contests which reduce the terms themselves to little more than slogans and epithets. A similar fate may well await the pair of terms to be introduced here. But for the time being the fact that they are rather new, or at least newly employed within an educational context, should prevent that.

In brief, I contend in this chapter that two distinguishably different ways of thinking about education and of translating that thought into practice undergird most of the differences of opinion that have circulated within educational circles over the past two or three centuries. Framed within an argument, which is how they are usually encountered, each of these two outlooks seeks to legitimate its own vision of how education should be conducted. It does so by promoting certain goals and practices, making them seem proper and just, while ignoring others or calling them into question.

These dichotomous orientations are not the exact opposites of which Protagoras spoke, though they are often presented that way by people propounding one or the other. How they *are* related to each other is a question I will consider in some detail in the second half of this chapter. For now, however, it will suffice to call their relationship enigmatic. Most of the time their challengers and defenders are depicted at swords' points, but there is a perspective from which the two outlooks appear complementary and interdependent. Indeed, there are angles of vision from which what originally seemed to be two diametrically opposed orientations suddenly appear to be one.

What shall we name these two points of view? As the chapter title already reveals, I recommend they be called the "mimetic" and the "transformative." I also propose we think of them not simply as two viewpoints on educational matters but as two traditions within the domain of educational thought and practice. Why *traditions*? Because each has a long and respectable history going back at least several hundred years and possibly beyond. Also, each is more than an intellectual argument. Each provokes feelings of partisanship and loyalty toward a particular point of view; each also entails commitment to a set of related practices. In short, each comprises what might be called (following Wittgenstein[1]) a "form of life," a relatively coherent and unified way of thinking, feeling, and acting within a particular domain—in this instance, the sphere of education. The term "traditions" stands for that complexity. Its use reminds us that each outlook stretches back in time, and that each has a "lived" dimension that makes it something much more than a polemical argument.

---

[1] Ludwig Wittgenstein, *Philosophical Investigations* (Oxford: Basil Blackwell, 1968) p. 9e.

The Mimetic Tradition

We turn to the "mimetic" tradition first not because it is any older or any more important than the one called "transformative," but principally because it is the easier of the two to describe. In addition, it is closer to what most people today seem to think education is all about. Thus, presenting it first has the advantage of beginning with the more familiar and moving to the less familiar. Third, it is more harmonious with all that is thought of as "scientific" and "rigorous" within education than is its competitor. To all who rank that pair of adjectives highly, as I reservedly do myself, therein lies an additional reason for putting it first.

This tradition is named "mimetic" (the root term is the Greek word *mimesis*, from which we get "mime" and "mimic") because it gives a central place to the transmission of factual and procedural knowledge from one person to another, through an essentially *imitative* process. If I had to substitute another equally unfamiliar word in its place, with which to engage in educational debate, I would choose "epistemic"—yet another derived from the Greek, this from *episteme*, meaning knowledge. The first term stresses the *process* by which knowledge is commonly transmitted, the second puts its emphasis on the *content* of the transaction. Thus we have the "mimetic" or the "epistemic" tradition; I prefer the former if for no other reason than that it places the emphasis where I believe it belongs, on the importance of *method* within this tradition.

The conception of knowledge at the heart of the mimetic tradition is familiar to most of us, though its properties may not always be fully understood even by teachers committed to this outlook on teaching. For this reason it seems essential to say something about its properties.

First of all, knowledge of a "mimetic" variety, whose transmission entails mimetic procedures, is by definition identifiable in advance of its transmission. This makes it secondhand knowledge, so to speak, not in the pejorative sense of that term, but simply in that it has to have belonged to someone first before it can belong to anyone else. In short, it is knowledge "presented" to a learner, rather than "discovered" by him or her.[2]

---

[2] Aristotle once remarked that "All instruction given or received by way of argument proceeds from pre-existent knowledge." (*Posterior Analytic*, Book I, 71a) By this he meant that we must begin with major and minor premises whose truth is beyond dispute before we can move to a novel conclusion. This is not quite the same as claiming that all knowledge is secondhand, but it does call attention to how much of the "known" is properly described as having been "transmitted" or "passed along" to students from teachers or teacher surrogates, such as textbooks or computers.

Such knowledge can be "passed" from one person to another or from a text to a person; we can thus see it as "detachable" from persons *per se*, in two ways. It is detachable in the first place in that it can be preserved in books and films and the like, so that it can "outlive" all who originally possessed it. It is detachable, secondly, in the sense that it can be forgotten by those who once knew it. Though it can be "possessed," it can also be "dispossessed" through memory loss. Moreover, it can be "unpossessed" in the sense of never having been "possessed" in the first place. A correlate of its detachability is that it can be "shown" or displayed by its possessor, a condition that partially accounts for our occasional reference to it as "objective" knowledge.

A crucial property of mimetic knowledge is its reproducibility. It is this property that allows us to say it is "transmitted" from teacher to student or from text to student. Yet when we speak of it that way we usually have in mind a very special kind of process. It does not entail handing over a bundle of some sort as in an actual "exchange" or "giving." Rather, it is more like the transmission of a spoken message from one person to another or the spread of bacteria from a cold-sufferer to a new victim. In all such instances both parties wind up possessing what was formerly possessed by only one of them. What has been transmitted has actually been "mirrored" or "reproduced" without its ever having been relinquished in the process.

The knowledge involved in all transmissions within the mimetic tradition has an additional property worth noting: It can be judged right or wrong, accurate or inaccurate, correct or incorrect on the basis of a comparison with the teacher's own knowledge or with some other model as found in a textbook or other instructional materials. Not only do judgments of this sort yield a measure of the success of teaching within this tradition, they also are the chief criterion by which learning is measured.

My final remark about knowledge as conceived within the mimetic tradition may already be obvious from what has been said. It is that mimetic knowledge is by no means limited to "bookish" learning, knowledge expressible in words alone. Though much of it takes that form, it also includes the acquisition of physical and motor skills, knowledge to be *performed* in one way or another, usually without any verbal accompaniment whatsoever. "Knowing that" and "knowing how" is the way the distinction is sometimes expressed.[3]

---

[3] For a well-known discussion of that distinction, see Gilbert Ryle, *The Concept of Mind* (New York: Barnes and Noble, 1949).

Here then are the central epistemological assumptions associated with the mimetic tradition. The key idea is that some kind of knowledge or skill can be doubly possessed, first by the teacher alone (or the writer of the textbook or the computer program), then by his or her student. In more epigrammatic terms, the slogan for this tradition might well be: "What the teacher (or textbook or computer) knows, that shall the student come to know."

How might the goal of this tradition be achieved? In essence, the procedure for transmitting mimetic knowledge consists of five steps, the fourth of which divides in two alternate routes, "a" or "b," dependent on the presence or absence of student error. The series is as follows:

Step One: *Test.* Some form of inquiry, either formal or informal, is initiated to discover whether the student(s) in question already knows the material or can perform the skill in question. This step is properly omitted if the student's lack of knowledge or skill can be safely assumed.

Step Two: *Present.* Finding the student ignorant of what is to be learned, or assuming him or her to be so, the teacher "presents" the material, either discursively—with or without the support of visual aids—or by modeling or demonstrating a skillful performance or some aspect thereof.

Step Three: *Perform/Evaluate.* The student, who presumably has been attentive during the presentation, is invited or required to repeat what he or she has just witnessed, read, or heard. The teacher (or some surrogate device, such as a test scoring machine) monitors the student's performance, making a judgment and sometimes generating a numerical tally of its accuracy or correctness.

Step Four (A): (Correct performance) *Reward/Fix.* Discovering the performance to be reasonably accurate (within limits usually set in advance), the teacher (or surrogate device) comments favorably on what the student has done and, when deemed necessary, prescribes one or more repetitions in order to habituate or "fix" the material in the student's repertoire of things known or skills mastered.

Step Four (B): (Incorrect performance) *Enter Remedial Loop.* Discovering the student's performance to be wrong (again within limits usually established in advance), the teacher (or surrogate) initiates a remedial procedure designed to correct the error in question. Commonly this procedure begins with a diagnosis of the student's difficulty followed by the selection of an appropriate corrective strategy.

Step Five: *Advance.* After the unit of knowledge or skill has been "fixed" (all appropriate corrections having been made and drills undertaken), the teacher and student advance to the next unit of "fresh" instruction, returning to Step One, if deemed necessary by the teacher, and repeating the moves in sequential order. The sequence of steps is repeated until the student has mastered all the prescribed knowledge or until all efforts to attain a prescribed level of mastery have been exhausted.

In skeletal form, this is the way instruction proceeds within the mimetic tradition. Readers familiar with cybernetic models will readily recognize the five steps outlined as an instance of what is commonly referred to as a "feedback loop" mechanism, an algorithmic device equipped with "internal guidance circuitry."[4]

Which teachers teach this way? Almost all do so on occasion, yet not all spend an equal amount of time at it. Some teachers work within the mimetic tradition only on weekends, figuratively speaking, about as often as a "do-it-yourself-er" might wield a hammer or turn a wrench. Others employ the same techniques routinely on a day-to-day basis, as might a professional carpenter or mechanic.

Which do which? That question will be treated at some length later in this chapter, where I will take up the relationship between the two traditions. For now it will suffice to observe in passing what is perhaps obvious, that teachers intent upon the transmission of factual information, plus those seeking to teach specific psychomotor skills, would more likely use mimetic procedures than would those whose conception of teaching involved educational goals less clearly epistemic in nature.

What might the latter category of goals include? To answer that question we must turn to the second of the two dominant outlooks within educational thought and practice, which I have chosen to call:

THE TRANSFORMATIVE TRADITION

The adjective "transformative" describes what this tradition deems successful teaching to be capable of accomplishing: a transformation of one kind or another in the person being taught—a qualitative change often of dramatic proportion, a metamorphosis, so

---

[4] See, for example, G.A. Miller, E. Galanter, and K.H. Pribham, *Plans and the Structure of Behavior* (New York: Holt, 1960).

to speak. Such changes would include all those traits of character and of personality most highly prized by the society at large (aside from those having to do solely with the possession of knowledge *per se*). They also would include the eradication or remediation of a corresponding set of undesirable traits. In either case, the transformations aimed for within this tradition are typically conceived of as being more deeply integrated and ingrained within the psychological makeup of the student—and therefore as perhaps more enduring— than are those sought within the mimetic or epistemic outlook, whose dominant metaphor is one of "adding on" to what already exists (new knowledge, new skills, etc.) rather than modifying the would-be learner in some more fundamental way.

What traits and qualities have teachers working within the transformative tradition sought to modify? Our answer depends on when and where we look. Several centuries ago, for example, when the mission of schools was primarily religious, what was being sought was nothing other than students' salvation through preparing them for Bible reading and other religiously oriented activities. Such remains the goal of much religious instruction today, though the form of its expression may have changed somewhat.

Over the years, as schooling became more widespread and more secular in orientation, educators began to abandon the goal of piety *per se*, and focused instead upon effecting "transformation" of character, morals, and virtue. Many continue to speak that way today, though it is more common to name "attitudes," "values," and "interests" as the psychological traits many of today's teachers seek to modify.

However one describes the changes sought within the transformative tradition, it is interesting that this undertaking is usually treated as more exalted or noble than the more mimetic type of teaching. Why this should be so is not readily apparent, but the different degrees of seriousness attached to the two traditions are apparent in the metaphors associated with each of them.

As I have already said, within the mimetic tradition knowledge is conceived of as something akin to material goods. Like a person materially wealthy, the possessor of knowledge may be considered "richer" than his ignorant neighbor. Yet, like the materially rich and poor, the two remain fundamentally equal as human beings. This metaphor of knowledge as coins in one's purse is consonant with the concomitant belief that it is "detachable" from its owner, capable of being "shown," "lost," and so forth. A related metaphor, one often used to lampoon the mimetic tradition, depicts the learner as a kind of vessel into which knowledge is "poured" or "stored." What is important about all such metaphors is that the vessel in question remains essentially unchanged, with or without its "contents."

The root image within the transformative tradition is entirely different. It is much closer to that of a potter working with clay than it is to someone using the potter's handiwork as a container for whatever contents such a vessel might hold. The potter, as we know, not only leaves her imprint on the vessel itself in the form of a signature of some kind, she actually molds and shapes the object as she creates it. All who later work with the finished product have a different relationship to it entirely. They may fill it or empty it to their hearts' content. They may even break it if they wish. But all such actions accept the object in question as a "given," something whose essence is fundamentally sacrosanct.

The metaphor of teacher-as-artist or teacher-as-creator gives the transformative tradition an air of profundity and drama, perhaps even spirituality, that is largely lacking within the mimetic tradition, whose root metaphor of mere addition of knowledge or skill is much more prosaic. But metaphors, as we know, are mere figures of speech. No matter how flattering they might be, they don't tell us whether such flattery is deserved. They leave us to ask whether teachers working within the transformative tradition actually succeed in doing what they and others sometimes boast they can do. And that's not all they leave unanswered. Beyond the question of whether transformative changes due to pedagogical interventions really occur at all there awaits the more practical question of *how* they happen. What do teachers do to bring them about? As we might guess, it is easier to answer the former question than the latter.

Fictional accounts of teachers who have had enduring effects on their students of the kind celebrated within the transformative tradition are familiar enough to be the stock in trade of the pedagogical novel. *Goodbye, Mr. Chips* and *The Prime of Miss Jean Brodie*[5] are but two of such works that come to mind most readily. Each exemplifies a teacher who has a profoundly transformative influence on his or her students. But what of real life? Do teachers *there* make a difference of the same magnitude as do the fictional Chipses and Brodies?

An answer to that question which I find quite convincing is contained in a study undertaken by Anne Kuehnle, a student of mine

---

[5] James Hilton, *Goodbye Mr. Chips* (Boston: Little, Brown and Co., 1934) and Muriel Spark, *The Prime of Miss Jean Brodie* (Philadelphia: Lippincott, 1961).

a few years back. In preparation for her term paper in a course on the analysis of teaching, work which later became the basis of her master's thesis, Kuehnle distributed questionnaires to 150 friends and neighbors in her hometown of Elmhurst, Illinois; she asked them to write a paragraph or two about the teachers they remembered most vividly. The results were striking. Not only did most respondents comply enthusiastically with the request, their descriptions yielded literally scores of vignettes showing the transformative tradition in action. Here are but three of them, chosen almost at random.

> He moved the learning process from himself to us and equipped us to study independently. We were able to see such mundane concepts as money supply, price mechanism, supply and demand, all around us. We became interested. We actually talked economics after class! In Eckstein's class I became aware that I was there to evaluate, not ingest, concepts. I began to discriminate . . .

> She was, to me, a glimpse of the world beyond school and my little town of 800 people. She was beautiful, vivacious, witty, and had a truly brilliant mind. Her energy knew no limits—she took on all the high school English classes, class plays, yearbook, began interpretive reading and declamatory contests, started a library in the town, and on and on. *She* was our town's cultural center.

> His dedication rubbed off on nearly all of us. I was once required to write him a 12-page report, and I handed in an 84-page research project. I always felt he deserved more than the minimum.[6]

These three examples are quite representative of the protocols quoted throughout Kuehnle's report. So if we can trust what so many of her respondents told us—and I am inclined to do so, for had I been asked I would have responded much as they did—there seems no shortage of testimonial evidence to support the conclusion that at least some teachers do indeed modify character, instill values, shape attitudes, generate new interests, and succeed in "transforming," profoundly and enduringly, at least some of the students in their charge. The question now becomes: How do they do it? How are such beneficial outcomes accomplished?

As most teachers will readily testify, the answer to that question will disappoint all who seek overnight to become like the teachers described in Kuehnle's report. It seems there *are* no formulas for

---

[6] Anne Kuehnle, "Teachers remembered," unpublished master's thesis, University of Chicago, June 1984.

accomplishing these most impressive if not miraculous feats of pedagogical skill. There are neither simple instructions for the neophyte nor complicated ones for the seasoned teacher. There is not even an epigram or two to keep in mind as guides for how to proceed, nothing analogous to the ancient "advice" that tells us to feed a cold and starve a fever.

And yet that last point is not quite as accurate as were the two that came before it. For if we look carefully at what such teachers do and listen to what others say about their influence, we begin to see that they *do* have some characteristic ways of working after all, "modes of operation" that, even if they can't be reduced to recipes and formulas, are worth noting all the same. The three of these modes most readily identifiable seem to me to be:

1. *Personal modeling.* Of the many attributes associated with transformative teaching, the most crucial ones seem to concern the teacher as a person. For it is essential to success within that tradition that teachers who are trying to bring about transformative changes personify the very qualities they seek to engender in their students. To the best of their ability they must be living exemplars of certain virtues or values or attitudes. The fulfillment of that requirement achieves its apex in great historical figures, like Socrates and Christ, who epitomize such a personal model; but most teachers already know that no attitude, interest, or value can be taught except by the teacher who himself or herself believes in, cares for, or cherishes whatever it is that he or she holds out for emulation.

2. *"Soft" suasion.* Among teachers working toward transformative ends, the "showing" and "telling" so central to the mimetic tradition (actions contained in Step Two: *Present* of the methodological paradigm outlined above) are replaced by less emphatic assertions and by an altogether milder form of pedagogical authority. The teaching style is rather more forensic and rhetorical than it is one of proof and demonstration. Often the authority of the teacher is so diminished by the introduction of a questioning mode within this tradition that there occurs a kind of role reversal, almost as though the student were teaching the teacher. This shift makes the transformative teacher look humbler than his or her mimetic counterpart, but it is by no means clear that such an appearance is a trustworthy indicator of the teacher's true temperament.

3. *Use of narrative.* Within the transformative tradition "stories" of one kind or another, which would include parables, myths, and

other forms of narrative, play a large role. Why this should be so is not immediately clear, but it becomes so as we consider what is common to the transformations that the schools seek to effect. The common element, it turns out, is their moral nature. Virtues, character traits, interests, attitudes, values—as educational goals all of them fall within the moral realm of the "right" or "proper" or "just." Now when we ask about the function or purpose of narrative, one answer (some might say the only one) is: to moralize.[7] Narratives present us with stories about how to live (or how not to live) our lives. Again, Socrates and Christ come readily to mind as exemplars of the teacher-as-storyteller as well as the teacher about whom stories are told.

The examples of Socrates and Christ as both transformative models and as storytellers help us to realize that differences in the conception of teaching within the two traditions go far beyond the question of what shall be taught and how it shall be done. They extend to the psychological and epistemological relationship between the teacher and his or her students.

Within the mimetic tradition the teacher occupies the role of expert in two distinct ways. He or she supposedly is in command of a specifiable body of knowledge or set of skills whose properties we have already commented upon. Such knowledge constitutes what we might call *substantive* expertise. At the same time the teacher is thought to possess the know-how whereby a significant portion of his or her substantive knowledge may be "transmitted" to students. The latter body of knowledge, whose paradigmatic contours have also been sketched, constitutes what we might call the teacher's *methodological* expertise. The students, by way of contrast, might be described as doubly ignorant. They neither know what the teacher knows, substantively speaking, nor do they know how to teach it in methodological terms. This dual condition of ignorance places them below the teacher epistemologically no matter where they stand regarding other social attributes and statuses.

Within the transformative tradition, the superiority of the teacher's knowledge, whether substantive or methodological, is not nearly so clear-cut. Nor is the teacher's status in general vis-à-vis his

---

[7] See Hayden White, "The value of narrativity in the representation of reality," in W.J.T. Mitchell (ed.), *On Narrative* (Chicago: University of Chicago Press, 1981), 1–24. Also, John Gardner, *On Moral Fiction* (New York: Basic Books, 1978). Gardner points out that "the effect of great fiction is to temper real experience, modify prejudice, humanize." (p. 114)

or her students. Instead, the overall relationship between the two is often vexingly ambiguous if not downright upsetting to some students; it can even become so at times to teachers themselves. Nowhere are many of these ambiguities portrayed more dramatically than in the early Socratic dialogues of Plato.[8] In the person of Socrates we witness perhaps the most famous of all transformative teachers in action. He is also a teacher whose actions are often as puzzling as they are edifying.

Does Socrates know more than his students? Well of course he does, says commonsense, why else would so many seek him out for advice and confront him with the most profound of questions? Yet, as we know, Socrates rarely if ever answers the questions he is asked, often professing to know less about the answer than does the questioner himself. Is he feigning ignorance when he behaves that way? It is not always easy to tell, as we can gather from the frequent expressions of puzzlement on the part of those conversing with him. And what about his method? How canny is he as a teacher? Does he really know what he is doing every step of the way, or is he more or less bumbling along much of the time, never quite sure of where he is going or of how to get there? Again, it is hard to say for sure. There are times when he seems completely in control of the situation, but other times when he seems utterly confused about what to say or do next; he even goes so far as to say so. Finally, what shall we make of the social relationship between Socrates and his fellow Athenians? Where do they stand in relation to each other? That too is a difficult question to answer definitively. Certainly he was greatly revered by many of his followers—Plato, of course, chief among them. But he was just as obviously envied by some and actively disliked by others.

A fuller treatment of the complexities and ambiguities of the Socratic method is beyond the scope of this work.[9] However, the little

---

[8] See Edith Hamilton and Huntington Cairns (eds.), *The Collected Dialogues of Plato* (Princeton, New Jersey: Princeton University Press, 1961). See especially the *Charmides, Laches, Euthydemus, Protagoras, Gorgias,* and *Meno.*

[9] For a fuller treatment of these and other ambiguities having to do with Socrates' teaching style see Gregory Vlastos, "Introduction: The paradox of Socrates," in Gregory Vlastos (ed.), *The Philosophy of Socrates* (Notre Dame, Indiana: University of Notre Dame Press, 1980), 1–21. Several other essays in that volume treat specialized aspects of the subject, such as Socrates' use of the technique of *elenchus.* See also, W.K.C. Guthrie, *Socrates* (Cambridge: Cambridge University Press, 1971), especially "The ignorance of Socrates," pp. 122–129. Also, Gerasimos Xenophon Santas, *Socrates* (Boston: Routledge & Kegan Paul, 1979). An unusually enlightening essay on the Socratic method is contained in Leonard Nelson, *Socratic Method and Critical Philosophy* (New York: Dover Publications, 1965), 1–40.

I have already said should make the point that ambiguities like those in the Socratic dialogues are common to the transformative tradition within teaching wherever it may be found. They are so because all such teachers are engaged in what is fundamentally *a moral undertaking* much like that of Socrates, whether they acknowledge it or not. Moreover, it is also a *philosophic* undertaking. That too is not always recognized by those actually engaged in such an enterprise.

What does it mean to speak of transformative teaching in these terms? In what sense is it either a moral or a philosophic undertaking? It is moral in that it seeks moral ends. Teachers working within the transformative tradition are actually trying to bring about changes in their students (and possibly in themselves as well) that make them better persons, not simply more knowledgeable or more skillful, but better in the sense of being closer to what humans are capable of becoming—more virtuous, fuller participants in an evolving moral order.

It is philosophic in that it employs philosophical means. No matter how else they might describe their actions, teachers working within the transformative tradition seek to change their students (and possibly themselves as well) by means neither didactic nor dogmatic. Instead, they use discussion, demonstration, argumentation. Armed only with the tools of reason, the transformative teacher seeks to accomplish what can be attained in no other way. Here is how one student of the process describes its operation within philosophy proper.

> We have discovered philosophy to be the sum total of those universal rational truths that become clear only through reflection. To philosophize, then, is simply to isolate these rational truths with our intellect and to express them in general judgments. . . .
>
> The teacher who seriously wishes to impart philosophical insight can aim only at teaching the art of philosophising. He can do no more than show his students how to undertake, each for himself, the laborious regress that alone affords insight into basic principles. If there is such a thing at all as instruction in philosophy, it can only be instruction in doing one's own thinking; more precisely, in the independent practice of the art of abstraction.[10]

Another commentator on the same subject sums up the difference by referring to himself as "a philosopher, not an expert." "The latter," he goes on to explain, "knows what he knows and what he does not

---

[10] Nelson, *Socratic Method*, 10–11.

know: the former does not. One concludes, the other questions—two very different language games."[11]

But talk of teachers being engaged in a moral and philosophic enterprise has its difficulties. For one thing, it sounds rather pretentious, especially when we consider some of the more mundane aspects of the average teacher's work—the routines of giving assignments, grading papers, taking attendance, keeping order in the classroom, and so on. Little of such activity deserves to be called either moral or philosophical. Moreover, teachers themselves do not seem to talk that way about what they do. Least of all do those who do it best, like Socrates.

The way out of these difficulties is to deny neither the moral and philosophical dimensions of teaching nor the prosaic nature of much that teachers actually do. Rather it requires that we acknowledge the compatibility of both viewpoints, seeing them as complementary rather than mutually exclusive. In short, nothing save a kind of conceptual narrow-mindedness keeps us from a vision of teaching as both a noble and a prosaic undertaking. Erasmus approached that insight several centuries ago when he remarked that "In the opinion of fools [teaching] is a humble task, but in fact it is the noblest of occupations."[12] Had he been a trifle more charitable he might have added that the fools were not totally wrong. Their trouble was that they were only half right.

Teachers themselves often overlook the moral dimensions of their work, but that failing must be treated as a problem to be solved, rather than as evidence of the amorality of teaching itself. There is no doubt that one can teach without giving thought to the transformative significance of what he or she is doing. But whether it should be so performed is another question entirely. Moreover, though the teacher may pay no attention whatsoever to such matters, we must ask if they are thereby eliminated as a class of outcomes. The well-known phenomenon of *unintended consequences*, sometimes referred to as "incidental learnings" when they take place within the context of a classroom, leads us to suspect that the delivery of moral messages and actions of transformative significance may often take place whether the teacher intends them to or not. Indeed, it is far more

---

[11] Jean-François Lyotard, *The Postmodern Condition: A Report on Knowledge* (Minneapolis: University of Minnesota Press, 1984), xxv.

[12] Claude M. Fuess and Emory S. Basford (eds.), *Unseen Harvests: A Treasury of Teaching* (New York: Macmillan, 1947): v.

interesting to ask whether such outcomes are inevitable, which is equivalent to asking whether all teachers are ultimately working within the transformative tradition whether they realize it or not.

That question turns us from a separate treatment of the two traditions to the relationship between them, a topic approachable either formally and abstractly or informally and concretely. The first approach asks, for example, whether one tradition is more rudimentary than the other in some logical sense. The second inquires how their relationship works in the real world, for example, how they are distributed among types of schools or school subjects or from one historical epoch to another. Both approaches are worth pursuing, but the more concrete one seems the more accessible of the two to start with.

I can answer the question of how these two traditions relate in the real world by observing initially that they don't get sorted out very clearly at all. There are few, if any, instances of either purely mimetic or purely transformative teaching, a fact that poses an important theoretical problem to which we shall return.

The closest approximation to an unadulterated version of transformative teaching in action that I can think of is probably to be found in the office of a psychotherapist or psychoanalyst where the focus of the therapeutic session (which is, after all, a form of pedagogy) is exclusively on matters related to the patient's personal thoughts and feelings. Certain kinds of religious counseling probably come a close second, for there too the goal is often exclusively one of alleviating discomfort of one kind or another. In both instances the "teacher" does not aim to transmit any subject matter in particular, at least none that could have been objectively defined in advance. Instead, what he or she seeks is an altered condition on the part of the "student"—in a word, a transformation.

Teaching that is solely mimetic in orientation may be as rare as that which is solely transformative, for transformative outcomes may occur whether they are intended or not.[13] At the same time, I can more easily imagine the former than the latter. The examples of close to pure mimetic teaching that come most readily to mind all include rudimentary skill instruction, such as dancing lessons or the teaching

---

[13] Some mimetic outcomes may be unintended. Consider the fact that students are sometimes able to imitate their teachers exactly, without the latter intending that to happen. Commonly, however, memory residue that is not "officially" sanctioned as a goal or objective within the mimetic lesson plan is not counted as "outcome."

of typing, but lectures whose content was intended to be purely informational might come just as close to being as exclusively mimetic as teaching ever gets.

But once we have acknowledged how rare it is to witness either type of teaching in isolation, we must observe that it is not at all uncommon for one or the other of the two traditions to predominate in various teaching situations, nor for one of them to do so typically in situations of a particular type. Three generalizations about this observation are worth mentioning. The first is that certain school subjects are more closely associated with either the transformative or the mimetic tradition than are others. Here C.P. Snow's much publicized distinction between the humanities and the sciences—the Two Cultures, as he called them—comes readily to mind. The correlation is by no means perfect, but it is close enough to sustain the stereotype that the teacher of science is principally concerned with the transmission of principles and facts—a mimetic mission, in the main—and the teacher of the humanities is occupied with concerns that I call here transformative.[14]

Secondly, we must also note that some curricular programs seem either more mimetic or transformative than others. We have only to compare programs in the liberal arts with their emphasis on cultural "well-roundedness" and those in vocational areas with their emphasis on "marketable skills." Once again, the correlation is by no means perfect but it is sufficient to sustain a widespread way of thinking about what such differences entail.

Third, some levels of schooling seem intrinsically more susceptible to the appeal of one tradition or the other. Educators who work with young children, for example, seem more naturally drawn toward the transformative tradition as a framework for their undertaking than do those who work with mature adults. The exceptions are many, of course, but the tendency is there all the same.

The trouble with all three of these generalizations is that none of

---

[14] In this connection it is worth noting that the psychologist Jerome Bruner posits the existence of "two irreducible modes of cognitive functioning—or more simply, two modes of thought" which he calls "the narrative and the paradigmatic." The latter conforms most closely to scientific thought and the former to humanistic studies. See Jerome Bruner, "Narrative and paradigmatic modes of thought," in Elliot Eisner (ed.), *Learning and Teaching the Ways of Knowing*, Eighty-fourth Yearbook of the National Society for the Study of Education, Part 2 (Chicago: University of Chicago Press, 1985), 97–115. A similar division is central to the work of Liam Hudson. See his *Frames of Mind* (London: Methuen, 1968). Also see, his *The Cult of the Fact* (London: Jonathan Cape, 1972).

them is very strong. Exceptions, I repeat, are plentiful. Who has not heard, for example, of the English teacher who customarily emphasizes nothing but facts and thereby snuffs out a love of literature before it has had a chance to develop? Or the math teacher whose concern for her students extends far beyond their ability to manipulate numbers? And what about the second or third grade teacher who concentrates on teaching the Three R's to the exclusion of all else? Or the teacher of adults who characteristically worries about the moral or motivational consequences of his or her actions? Are not all of these plausible contradictions of the above generalizations? They are indeed. More than that, they are highly probable as well, which is why we must treat such generalizations with care.

Moreover, the likely exceptions to those generalizations also make us realize that most if not all teaching situations can operate to some degree within either dominant tradition. In other words, they can be shaped to serve either the mimetic or the transformative tradition or some combination thereof, depending in part on the predilections of individual teachers but also depending on things like the prevailing climate of opinion, administrative policies, the teachings of ostensible experts in such matters, and so forth.[15]

The malleability of teaching, its capacity to be skewed, as it were, in either direction, toward dominance by either more mimetic or more transformative sets of concerns, leads us to ask in which direction the profession as a whole seems to be moving these days. It also prompts us to search for other overall tendencies beyond the three I have already mentioned.

My own reading of the direction in which teaching seems to be headed is more of an hypothesis than it is a conclusion about which I feel quite confident. At the same time I would describe it as more than a guess. Teaching within our own country and possibly within the Western world at large seems to be moving in the direction of becoming increasingly mimetic in its orientation and, correspondingly, less transformative. Moreover, I suspect the drift in this direction has been going on for generations, if not centuries.

What are the signs that the influence of the mimetic tradition is on the increase and the transformative one in decline? A few seem fairly obvious to me, others are less so. Among the former, I am most struck by the gradual turning away of educators in general from that

---

[15] Similarly, Bruner points out that a narrative can be translated into a paradigmatic mode in the same way that a story can be told of a scientific discovery. Bruner, "Narrative and paradigmatic modes of thought," p. 113.

broad set of transformative goals that over the years have been called character, moral development, deportment, good conduct, and citizenship. This is not to say that all such terms have disappeared completely from the lexicon of educators. Indeed, a few of them seem to be enjoying something of a revival these days.[16] However, it seems to me incontrovertible that today's public schools are far less engaged in trying to shape and mold what today might be called the personality of their students than was true a generation or two ago. In current discussions of what our schools are all about talk of morality and character has been replaced by notions like mastery, basic skills, competency, and accountability. That shift in the language of educational goals and purposes is the most clear-cut sign of the move toward the mimetic tradition.

A far more subtle sign, though no less telling perhaps, is the gradual emergence and the ultimate hegemony of a "scientific spirit" within the educational community at large, particularly among its leadership, whether in universities or in high administrative positions. Educational research in general and the educational testing movement in particular are two of the more obvious expressions of that spirit. Each in its way constitutes a challenge to the transformative tradition through its endorsement of greater precision, objectivity, and reliability in the conduct of educational affairs.

As evidence of the power and pervasiveness of this "scientific" outlook within the educational research community in particular, witness the fact that most research on teaching focuses on the teaching of those school subjects most infused with a mimetic outlook—reading skills, mathematics and the sciences. Also note that achievement test scores have become *the* outcome variable by which to measure teaching effectiveness and the quality of schools in general, not only for researchers and many school administrators but for the public at large.

What are we to make of the trend as described? The answer to this broad question will depend in turn on how we respond to two narrower sets of queries, one whose focus is essentially causal, the other evaluative. The first asks how we explain the phenomenon in question. What seems to be causing it? Is it limited to the field of education or does it extend to other social institutions as well? The second asks how we should greet it. Should we be pleased or alarmed

---

[16] Moral development, in particular, seems to be back in vogue of late as the result of the studies of Kohlberg and his followers at Harvard. The "value clarifications" movement, spurred by the late Louis Raths, is another attempt to revitalize the interest of educators in what are essentially transformative ends.

by the gradual ascendence of the mimetic tradition, if such indeed is really happening? Should we seek to promote, retard, or perhaps even reverse what seem to be today's trends? Are any or all such options ours to start with? Are they at all realistic? I cannot promise to answer either set of questions in the following discussion. Instead I will try to chart the direction of future investigations for myself and others by exploring lines of inquiry that seem at this stage of our knowledge to be potentially fruitful.

In response to the first set of causal questions, I will posit the interconnectedness of educational phenomena on the one hand and broad social trends on the other and urge that we trace those linkages with as much precision and thoroughness as possible. This seems the most sensible line of investigation to start with for at least two reasons. The first is that we naturally expect what goes on in our schools and in the minds and hearts of teachers to be influenced by events and ideas that originate beyond the classroom walls. We do so because such lines of influence are abundantly evident in almost every phase of the schools' operation. We sometimes complain and perhaps rightly so, that the school is isolated as an institution and resistant to the forces of change buffeting it from the outside.[17] But there is no doubt that the school is responsive to external conditions in any number of ways, from the content of the curriculum to the design of school architecture. This being so, it seems perfectly reasonable to anticipate that even something as exclusively pedagogical (or seemingly so) as a "tradition of teaching" will not be immune to influence from the outside. Thus we have the first reason for positing a strong linkage between conditions within our schools and the larger society.

Furthermore, certain connections between the mimetic or the transformative tradition on the one hand, and broader social phenomena on the other, fairly cry out for recognition and acknowledgement at the start without the need of an elaborate investigative undertaking. I do not deny that we need to know much more about such linkages, but I do believe that the place to initiate one or two lines of investigation seems fairly obvious.

The two that stand out most obviously to me are the linkage between the mimetic tradition and the emergence of a scientific/technological world view on the one hand, and that between the transformative tradition and the methods of Socrates on the other. Each of these connections in turn points to a deeper linkage between

---

[17]See, for example, Seymour Sarason, *The Culture of School and the Problem of Change* (Boston: Allyn and Bacon, 1971 [Revised 1982]).

both traditions and a set of historical controversies whose echoes continue to reverberate across the centuries.

The first controversy, preserved chiefly in the Platonic dialogues, is between Socrates and the group of men usually referred to as the Sophists.[18] The issue separating Socrates and his Sophistic antagonists were far too numerous and complicated to go into here in any detail.[19] Chief among them, however, were the questions of what it meant to be a teacher and what it was possible for a teacher to accomplish. In particular, the question of whether virtue can be taught occupied many of their discussions. The professional status of teaching was also an issue between them, for the Sophists commonly accepted fees for their services whereas Socrates himself reportedly never did so.

Perhaps I read too much into a set of two-thousand-year-old disputes to see in them the seeds of some of today's disagreements about teaching and how it should be conducted. But such is my own impression whenever I reflect upon the pedagogical significance of those ancient arguments, particularly the ones in the earlier dialogues such as *Protagoras* and *Meno*. To me, whether he is arguing with a famous Sophist like Protagoras or merely conversing with one or more young men of Athens, Socrates emerges characteristically as a living example of the transformative teacher, or at least of one important variant within that tradition. His Sophistic antagonists, on the other hand, usually seem to me closer to what I have called the mimetic tradition in both manner and content of their teaching.

Socrates personifies the seeker after truth. He himself professes to possess precious little knowledge about most things, except of course for that crucial nugget of negative knowledge, of knowing that he does not know. Thus he appears to have very little to teach students in the way of facts or principles or even skills. In no way could he be described as the kind of teacher we today would call "a subject-matter specialist." He was simply a humble man. Yet his humility with respect to the possession of knowledge made him the strangest of creatures in the eyes of many of his contemporaries, as it might do so today were he suddenly to reappear among us. An *ignorant* teacher? What a contradiction in terms!

But Socrates' ignorance, as readers of the dialogues also know,

---

[18] These included, among others, Protagoras, Gorgias, Hippias, Prodicus, Cratylus, and Thrasymachus.

[19] For a full exposition of the topic see W.K.C. Guthrie, *The Sophists* (Cambridge: Cambridge University Press, 1971). Also see G.B. Kerferd, *The Sophistic Movement* (Cambridge: Cambridge University Press, 1981).

was not always as great as he pretended, not even about matters far removed from the ordinary. Moreover, it did not extend to all forms of knowledge; nor did his attitude of humility. He is portrayed as being supremely confident, almost arrogantly so at times, when it comes to knowing two things: what kind of knowledge to seek and how to seek it.

To judge by his discussions, the knowledge that Socrates thought most worth seeking was, in a word, moral. At a superficial level it was knowledge most directly concerned with the meaning of key terms like virtue and justice and piety. But indirectly and at a more profound level it had to do with how humans should conduct their lives. It was not knowledge of the physical world, though Socrates clearly respected that form of knowing as well, nor was it the kind of knowledge that could readily be put to work in the marketplace or the political forum, though he speaks respectfully of that too. It was moral knowledge that he was chiefly concerned with, knowledge with the power to transform the lives of those possessing it.

Socrates also believed that the only path to the knowledge he sought was the arduous one of persistent inquiry through conversations with fellow seekers after the truth. Within those conversations questions were invariably given a higher priority than were answers, which may partially explain why so few answers were ever forthcoming. But, strangely enough, their absence in no way detracts from the pedagogical impact of the exercise, both upon the actors within the scene (Socrates included) and upon the reader as witness. Almost all are changed by the experience, it seems, sometimes in ways not easy to fathom.[20] It is this capacity to transfix his audience, to awaken

---

[20] Those who engage in intellectual exchanges with Socrates often depart in a frustrated and angry mood. In fact, it is frequently obvious that Socrates is not playing fair with his opponents. One well-known scholar of the Socratic method summarizes some of the more unsavory qualities of the master's performance:

It is plain that Socrates, besides being an original and powerful mind, was also something of an intellectual clown, a reveler in circus debate, a diabolical needler of his contemporaries. He is constantly on stage, in the agora, gymnasia and wrestling schools, festivals, dinner parties, the courtyards of great houses. He chooses his antagonists, fixes the subject, makes sure he has the attention of the audience, invites his opponent to speak his mind freely and without fear, elicts from him an opinion, a speech, a dogma, and then proceeds to counterpunch the poor man and his opinion to death, mixing in his blows not only philosophical points and arguments but also sarcasm, irony that borders on insincerity, and personal insults; and he does not rest until he has extracted from his victim a public confession of utter helplessness. At the end, when it is painfully obvious that his opponent will never recover, he

the idle thinker from his dogmatic slumber without at the same time lecturing him on what to think, that leads me to rank Socrates among the very first teachers to work almost exclusively within the transformative tradition.

The Sophists with whom Socrates had some of his most spirited exchanges held a very different attitude from his toward almost all aspects of knowledge and its acquisition and a quite different set of practices as well. Many of them, such as Hippias the polymath, not only professed to know a lot about many things, but took delight in flaunting their knowledge before others. In a word, they were boastful of what they knew. In addition, they put a price on their knowledge by charging fees for lessons, making it a commodity, something that could be bought and sold. Third, they proffered answers to questions, not questions themselves; therefore, their typical mode of instruction was one of telling, rather than querying. Fourth, what they promised as outcomes of their tutelage were the kinds of skills and knowledge that supposedly would pay off in worldly terms—the art of rhetoric, for example, a skill readily useful in the political arena. Finally, they were for the most part itinerant teachers whose contacts with their students were relatively short-lived and whose social relations with them were also rather businesslike and formal when compared with Socrates, a local citizen and familiar figure, beloved by a loyal company of young Athenians.

This quick sketch of some of the differences between the pedagogical approach of Socrates and that of the Sophistic movement in general is far too hastily drawn to yield but the roughest of overviews of a complex and intriguing topic. Moreover, not all of the differences

---

proposes that they all go home and start all over again another time. It is no wonder that he never has a second dialogue with the same man. [Gerasimos Xenophon Santas, *Socrates* (Boston: Routledge & Kegan Paul, 1979), 6.]

Whether the use of such tactics should count as demerits, so to speak, against Socrates' reputation as a teacher is a question well worth pondering. Certainly a teacher today who used the same approach would incur severe criticism from teaching colleagues and students alike. However, it is by no means clear that the same standards of social gentility applied in ancient Greece. Another Socratic scholar of note claims that Socrates suffered from what he calls "a failure of love." He continues:

In saying this I am not taking over-seriously the prickly exterior and the pugilist's postures. I have already argued that he does care for the souls of his fellows. But the care is limited and conditional. If men's souls are to be saved, they must be saved his way. And when he sees they cannot, he watches them go down the road to perdition with regret but without anguish. [Gregory Vlastos, "Introduction: The paradox of Socrates," in Gregory Vlastos (ed.), *The Philosophy of Socrates*, 16.]

mentioned bear directly on my earlier discussion of the distinction between the mimetic and transformative traditions. Nonetheless, even in as crude a sketch as this one, one can strongly sense Socrates moving in one pedagogical direction and most of his Sophistic opponents moving in another. It should further be apparent that the two directions set upon in those faraway days and that distant land are ones whose paths ultimately join (through what circuitous routes we can only begin to imagine) the two pedagogical traditions whose turns and twists form the double helix of educational thought that remains with us to this day.

I will turn now to the connection between the mimetic tradition and the emergence of a scientific/technological world view. My central point is not that mimetic teaching began with the Enlightenment or anything like that, for in an abbreviated way we have already traced its roots back to the Greeks. Rather it is that the idea of a social science, which was an outgrowth of the Enlightenment, gave an impetus to that tradition that sent it hurtling with enormous force into the modern era. It did so in a variety of ways.

One way was to foster the development of psychology—a mental science, as it was commonly referred to in the latter part of the nineteenth century, which quickly became the most scientific of the disciplines within the social sciences and the one to which educators most readily turned for help.[21] Nor were psychologists at all shy in responding to such pleas. As we saw in the case of William James, many were modest in the claims made on behalf of this fledgling field of study, but not all were as reticent as he in their modesty. Even if they were, they could not have restrained the mushrooming of a near insatiable desire for psychology's "findings" as they related to a wide variety of educational topics, from theories of how learning took place under normal conditions to questions of how to deal with various kinds of mental disabilities. As a result, it was not very long before the emergence of the subspecialty of *educational* psychology, whose research focus was to be exclusively on topics of concern to teachers and school administrators.[22] There soon followed the branching off of

---

[21] Recall, for example, the enthusiastic response to William James' *Talks to Teachers* described in Chapter 2.

[22] The first issue of the *Journal of Educational Psychology* appeared in January, 1910. For a critical reaction to the exaggerated hopes of E.L. Thorndike, one of America's first and most prominent educational psychologists, see Philip W. Jackson, "The promise of educational psychology," in Frank H. Farley and Neal J. Gordon (eds.), *Psychology and Education* (Berkeley, California: McCutchan Publishing Corporation, 1981), 389–405.

the more clinically oriented subspecialties of school psychology, counseling, and so forth, whose goal became not simply to investigate psychological phenomena of interest to educators and report their findings to practitioners, but to deliver psychological services directly within the schools.

What is important about this historical linkage between psychology and education is that almost from the start psychology was oriented in the direction of the mimetic tradition within teaching, as it continues to be today.[23] This orientation is an outgrowth of psychology's commitment to the goal of objectivity, its insistence on the importance of measurement, and its adherence to a reductionist's strategy of searching for the smallest possible unit of analysis—the psychological atom, so to speak. These add up to a focus on learning outcomes that can be measured with considerable precision, which means, in turn, those that conform to the epistemological outlook of the mimetic tradition.[24]

If we start with a conception of a helping relationship between psychology and education, with the latter dependent upon the former, it is but a short step to a bolder outlook (a dream perhaps) of education as a science in its own right. That too is part of the legacy of the Enlightenment. Its modern embodiment is the enterprise known as educational research.

Where psychological research ends and educational research begins is almost impossible to say. The two dovetail so neatly that many studies could as well be called one as the other. Yet it remains true that not all research in education draws upon psychological

---

[23] It is of course true that educational psychologists have also paid some attention to educational outcomes more closely associated with the transformative tradition than the mimetic, goals like moral development or the formation of personality traits. But let me make two observations about that more "balanced" view. First, imbalance typifies the usual state of affairs. The amount of psychological research focused on mimetic outcomes such as reading scores or achievement test data in math and science exceeds by a considerable magnitude the amount focused on the more transformative ends of schooling. Second, even when attention is given to what the schools are doing transformatively—as, for example, in some psychologists' recent surge of interest in the schools' possible role in moral development—the concern with measurement remains focal, requiring that what are essentially transformative goals be translated into the language of the mimetic tradition.

[24] Bruner remarks that psychology has traditionally focused on a mode of thought he calls "paradigmatic" while overlooking one that he calls "narrative." He refers to this imbalance as an "odd posture" and "a curious twist of history" and suggests that its explanation "is probably located in our longed-for proximity to the natural sciences." See Bruner, "Narrative and paradigmatic modes of thought," 102–103.

concepts and categories. The portion that does not covers a broad territory; it includes everything from studies of educational finance to investigations of school law, from cross-cultural comparisons of educational achievement to naturalistic observations of classroom life.

Within that vast domain of educational research lying outside the purely psychological the investigations most relevant to the topic at hand are obviously those that focus on teaching. Even this limited category contains quite an assortment. It includes studies of teaching at all levels of schooling and of almost every imaginable school subject. Methodologically, the investigations it covers span the gamut of data-gathering techniques, from the experimental and quasi-experimental to the informal and impressionistic. They vary in intent from the normative to the merely descriptive, from studies whose goal is the discovery of new and better teaching methods to those claiming to have no meliorative aim at all beyond trying to figure out "how teaching works."[25]

Yet within that vast assortment of studies several trends bearing upon the two traditions of teaching are clearly discernible. The first is that those teaching situations that get studied the most are ones in which mimetic goals predominate. I have already commented upon this regarding psychological research in education. The conditions responsible for this hold with equal force for educational research in general. There too is a strong tendency to study educational outcomes that are readily measurable by a written test of some kind—most commonly a standardized achievement test. What this means in terms of the curricular focus of such studies is that school subjects like math and science and reading get investigated far more often than do social studies or art or music. Moreover, even within those subjects most frequently studied the focus of the investigation is almost always upon *epistemic* outcomes rather than *transformative* ones—on the acquisition of scientific *knowledge* rather than the development of a scientific *attitude*, on the growth of reading *skills* rather than the cultivation of a love for literature.

A second characteristic of research on teaching too dominant to be called a mere trend is that most of its studies are normative rather than descriptive; that is, they are designed to come up with better ways of teaching rather than simply to describe or to understand

---

[25]Research on teaching has become so voluminous in the last half–century that even efforts to summarize it have produced a rather vast literature. To become acquainted with that literature, start with Merrill Wittrock, (ed.) *Third Handbook of Research on Teaching* (New York: Macmillan, 1985).

what teachers do and why they do it.[26] This state of affairs is perfectly natural in an applied field like education. Indeed, one might reasonably wonder why a person would want to undertake a purely descriptive study of teaching at all without the ulterior motive of unearthing something about the process that might possibly be improved.

But even though it may seem like the most natural thing in the world to do, searching for better ways of teaching through the instrumentality of research is not the value-neutral process that some researchers claim. Nor is it simply a way of serving the teaching profession by lending it a helping hand, as it is also sometimes portrayed.

For one thing, most such research concentrates almost exclusively on the observable aspects of teaching—on what teachers *do* and, moreover on what they can be seen to do fairly regularly and repeatedly. (Long stretches of observation are prohibitively time-consuming and expensive from the standpoint of both data collection and analysis, and also intrusive and disruptive of classroom routines.) Thus, the bulk of such research leans strongly in the direction of subsuming all of teaching under the single category of technique.

For another, the possibility of discovering the secret of good teaching through research means at least hypothetically that the researchers will possess that knowledge before teachers themselves will. Thus, they will be in a position to control and benefit from its release. This position of epistemic superiority need not be abused, of course, but there is always the danger it could be. Should that happen, as has been known in the past, the situation becomes one of "experts" controlling teachers from above as would a puppetmaster, talking down to them, doing all the things that William James warned against (and was partially guilty of himself, as we have already seen).

---

[26] For a somewhat different distinction between "normative" and "descriptive" research on teaching see Karen Kepler Zumwalt, "Research on teaching: policy implications for teacher education," in Ann Lieberman and Milbrey W. McLaughlin (eds.), *Policy Making in Education*, Eighty-first Yearbook of the National Society for the Study of Education, Part 1 (Chicago: University of Chicago Press, 1982), 215–248. Zumwalt points out that descriptive research can also be normative in the sense of its being used as the basis for prescriptive statements about how to teach. Her point is that all research yielding prescriptions about how to teach falls within what she calls "a technological orientation." The difficulty I have with this is that it seems to conjoin methodological and purposive categories. What she calls "process-product" research is also in my terms "descriptive" provided all it seeks to do is to describe. When research seeks to establish norms for action I look upon it as no longer descriptive, no matter what its methodology.

As should by now be clear, a purely technological conception of teaching, teaching-by-the-numbers we might call it, is far more likely to take root within the mimetic tradition, with its emphasis on both methodological and epistemological concerns, than it is within the transformative tradition, where both the method and content of teaching are much more vaguely defined. However, although it may more easily take root there, a technological and a mimetic orientation toward teaching are not one and the same; nor does *taking root* mean that it will necessarily *take over* in the sense of becoming the dominant perspective within that tradition. Whether that will happen, or indeed has already happened, is a question to be examined and not treated as a foregone conclusion. That question brings us near the close of this exploration of an important division within educational thought and practice, but it certainly does not close the door on further exploration of the topic, as will soon be clear.

What do others think about the mounting importance of the mimetic tradition? As might be expected, the answer depends on whom you ask. The more extreme advocates of the two traditions differentially perceive the trends I have described as either alarming or comforting.

Those who look upon the growth of the mimetic tradition as an unadulterated good or close to that, which in today's terms means those who most applaud innovations like mastery learning, competency testing, the teacher accountability movement, computerized instruction, and so on, doubtless see such changes as signs of progress, as helping to give a firmer intellectual foundation to the entire enterprise of education, and as moving it a step closer toward the ultimate goal of a pedagogical science. Many though not all those same people doubtless view the decline of the transformative tradition with equal delight. They believe it rids the teaching profession of unnecessary sentimentality and mystifying talk about vague notions like character and virtue and at the same time removes yet another roadblock toward making the practice of teaching more objective and precise and its results more measurable.[27]

---

[27] For a fair-minded presentation of what I would call "mimetic optimism" see N.L. Gage, *The Scientific Basis of the Art of Teaching* (New York: Teachers College Press, 1978). An updated version of the same argument appears in N.L. Gage, *Hard Gains in the Social Sciences: The Case of Pedagogy* (Bloomington, Indiana: Phi Delta Kappa Center on Evaluation, Development and Research, 1985). Also see Robert Glaser, *Adaptive Education: Individual Diversity and Learning* (New York: Holt, Rinehart and Winston, 1977). For my own reaction to Glaser's form of optimism see Philip W. Jackson, "Private lessons in public schools: remarks on the limits of adaptive instruction," in

Those who see the growth of mimetic teaching as regrettable do so, by linking it to the technological side of that tradition, by seeing in it all that is undesirable about the gradual encroachment of technology. In its extreme form the vision is one of widespread dehumanization, Orwellian in scope. "Bureautechnocracy" is the term given it by one pair of authors who explain the term as

> *a pattern of social management wherein the hierarchized, pyramidal, depersonalized model of human organization (bureaucracy) is linked with standardized, rationalized means (technology) with the overall aim of achieving control, flexibility, and efficiency in reaching some commercial or social objective.*[28]

There is an additional worry sometimes voiced in connection with the mimetic tradition in particular, though it can cover certain aspects of the transformative tradition as well. It is that students are differentially exposed to the two traditions on the basis of social class membership, a fact that itself constitutes a form of social injustice. What this charge declares in detail is that those practices most closely associated with the mimetic tradition—an emphasis on memorization, short answer tests, copying, drill, and recitation—are especially favored in schools and classrooms whose students come from predominantly if not exclusively poor and working-class families in underprivileged environments. Interestingly enough, though some of today's critics fail to recognize it, this situation appears to be at least a century or two old. One finds it lampooned in Dickens' *Hard Times* and commented upon in historical documents such as Matthew Arnold's reports on British school practices in the mid- to late-nineteenth century[29] and John Locke's plans for "pauper schools" more than a century earlier.[30]

Moreover, the charge goes beyond the accusation of differential exposure to the two traditions on the basis of social class. Not only are

---

Margaret C. Wang and Herbert J. Walberg (eds.), *Adapting Instruction to Individual Differences* (Berkeley, California: McCutchan Publishing Corporation, 1985). pp. 66–81. For Glaser's reply see Robert Glaser, "Cognition and adaptive education," in Wang and Walberg, 82–90.

[28] Charles A. Tesconi, Jr., and Van Cleve Morris, *The Anti-Man Culture: Bureautechnocracy and the Schools* (Urbana, Illinois: University of Illinois Press, 1972), 7. (Italics in original.)

[29] Fred G. Walcott, *The Origins of Culture and Anarchy: Matthew Arnold and Popular Education in England* (Toronto: University of Toronto Press, 1970), 13.

[30] See Robert Herbert Quick, *Essays on Educational Reformers* (New York: D. Appleton and Company, 1899), 219ff.

children from poor and working-class families the objects of more mimetically oriented practices, so critics inform, but they are often exposed to the worst of those practices. It is not just that they are asked to memorize more facts and copy material from textbooks that is troublesome, but that the facts they are asked to memorize and the material they are required to copy are themselves inferior, intellectually speaking, when compared with equivalent exercises in schools and classrooms that serve pupils from more affluent families.

The same criticism applies, as has already been suggested, to differences in the more transformatively oriented practices. Not only are they emphasized less in schools serving children from poor and working-class families, we are told, but when they are employed the focus is on the development of character traits such as docility and punctuality rather than those of inquisitiveness and intellectual aggressiveness.[31]

Why children of the poor should receive more than their share of mimetic teaching—and perhaps an inferior brand of it as well—is not hard to figure out once we begin to consider the constellation of conditions surrounding their education—the deprivations they suffer in other spheres as well, their widely publicized "learning difficulties," public attitudes concerning the "place" of the poor within our society, what they are said to "need," and so forth. What all these add up to is the belief that such children need more "drill and practice" than do those coming from more privileged homes, that they need more in the way of "the basics," that they need more practical training, which means courses that are more vocationally oriented and purport to develop so-called "marketable skills," and so on.

Such "needs" seem to square with the mimetic tradition's emphasis on the primacy of knowledge and its transmission. They also go well with that tradition's focus on method and technique. Small wonder that programs like "mastery learning," written systems of individualizing instruction, and other "by-the-numbers" schemes for regularizing and automating instruction—routines that are essentially mimetic in nature—are so often first tried out and adopted in schools serving children of the poor. That's where they are so obviously needed, or so common sense encourages us to believe.

Here then are the two extremes within the gradual encroachment of the mimetic tradition: a kind of naive optimism on the one hand

---

[31]Some evidence that this may be so appears in John Goodlad's *A Place Called School* (New York: McGraw-Hill, 1984). See also the companion volume by Jeannie Oakes, *Keeping Track* (New Haven: Yale University Press, 1985).

and a "gloom-and-doom" perspective on the other. Must we choose between them? I think not, or rather I hope not; yet my own optimism is tempered by two reservations. The first derives from my conviction that some worries that beset upholders of the transformative traditions are truly worth worrying about. Though I can't accept the lugubrious vision that teaching will be reduced to nothing but technique, leaving teachers to behave like a bunch of automatons controlled "from above," neither can I sanguinely dismiss such a prospect as being downright silly. I feel similarly about worries over the preponderance of mimetic procedures in schools and classrooms serving large numbers of children of the poor. Such fears may be exaggerated, but they seem to me worthy of investigation all the same.

The other consideration that undermines my middle-of-the-road optimism, making it rather weaker than I would like, is my inability to see how an effective synthesis between the two traditions can be achieved. In short, I fear that as polarities of educational thought the mimetic and the transformative will be with us for a long time to come, perhaps forever. Moreover, a certain amount of tension and strife between the two traditions may turn out to be inevitable. How to keep the tension within tolerable limits and therefore productive rather than destructive and, at the same time, how to avoid the attraction of extremes within each tradition are questions I cannot answer except by advocating the continued exercise of intelligence and goodwill in the search for answers.

At the start of the chapter I said that from certain angles of vision our two traditions, which so often are depicted as being diametrically opposed to one another, suddenly appear to be one. The image is tantalizing but in need of explanation, especially after the above comments about the prospect of continued tension and strife between the two traditions. What I had in mind in saying that the two can suddenly appear as one were those rare and memorable encounters with teachers that leave us doubly enriched, morally as well as intellectually—the kind of encounters that I suspect many of Anne Kuehnle's respondents were thinking of when they answered her questionnaire. I call them rare because I think they are for most people; I know they were for me. Moreover, I am not at all sure that most of us are sharply aware of them while they are happening (again, I know I wasn't), nor that the teachers themselves are always fully conscious of what they are doing and of the impact they are having on at least some of their students. Certainly few if any would describe themselves as achieving a blend of two pedagogical traditions, as I have credited them with doing. In fact, most of them doubtless would not know what we were talking about if they heard their achievement described in these terms. Like the man who discovered he had been speaking prose all his life, they would probably react with surprise and disbelief.

But what interests us here about such teachers is not how they would react to our descriptions of them but how their accomplishments tally with my observations of the unlikelihood of reconciliation between the two traditions. They do so in this way. Recall that I also announced at the start that some teachers seem to work within the mimetic tradition on weekends, so to speak, whereas others do so much more regularly. The same thing may of course be said about teachers working within the transformative tradition. There too we would expect to find part-timers as well as full-timers. When we consider what has already been said about those rare teachers who seem to achieve a near perfect blending of the mimetic and the transformative, we can see that the tension between the two traditions can be experienced individually as well as collectively. What it makes conceivable, if not exactly likely, is the possibility that such tensions may be more readily resolved at the individual level, within the confines of a single classroom, than at the level of public debate, where the rift between the traditions appears so great that one is virtually forced to choose sides. The public debates will doubtless continue as far into the future as one might care to gaze. Meanwhile, the question of what to do about such matters as we go about our work as teachers remains for each of us to ponder and decide.

INDEX

ABOUT THE AUTHOR

PHILIP W. JACKSON is the David Lee Shillinglaw Distinguished Service Professor of Education and the Behavioral Sciences at the University of Chicago, where he has taught since 1955. Mr. Jackson's interest in the study of teaching began in 1948, when he enrolled as a student at what was then the State Teachers College in Glassboro, New Jersey (now a State University). He received his Ph.D. from Teachers College, Columbia University, in 1954. In addition to college and university teaching, Mr. Jackson has also taught in the New Jersey public schools, and was Principal of the University of Chicago's Nursery School and Director of the University's Laboratory Schools. He is the author of *Life in Classrooms, Creativity and Intelligence* (with J.W. Getzels), and numerous monographs and articles in professional journals.